D0500415

THE MANHATTAN PROJECT AND THE ATOMIC BOMB IN AMERICAN HISTORY

Other titles *in American History*

IN
AMERICAN
HISTORY

THE MANHATTAN PROJECT AND THE ATOMIC BOMB IN AMERICAN HISTORY

Doreen Gonzales

Enslow Publishers, Inc.

40 Industrial Road   PO Box 38
Box 398   Aldershot
Berkeley Heights, NJ 07922 Hants GU12 6BP
USA   UK

http://www.enslow.com

Copyright © 2000 by Doreen Gonzales

All rights reserved.

No part of this book may be reproduced by any means
without the written permission of the publisher.

Library of Congress Cataloging-in-Publication Data

Gonzales, Doreen.
    The Manhattan Project and the atomic bomb in American history /
Doreen Gonzales.
        p. cm. — (In American history)
    Includes bibliographical references and index.
    Summary: Describes the events and people surrounding the creation of
the atomic bomb, and examines the effects of its use during World War II.
    ISBN 0-89490-879-0
    1. Manhattan Project (U.S.)—History Juvenile literature. 2. Atomic
bomb—United States—History Juvenile literature. [1. Manhattan Project
(U.S.) 2. Atomic bomb—History.] I. Title. II. Series.
QC773.3.U5G65   2000
355.8'25119'0973
                                                99-16690
                                                CIP

Printed in the United States of America

10 9 8 7 6 5 4

To Our Readers: We have done our best to make sure all Internet addresses in
this book were active and appropriate when we went to press. However, the
author and the publisher have no control over and assume no liability for the
material available on those Internet sites or on other Web sites they may link to.
Any comments or suggestions can be sent by e-mail to comments@enslow.com or
to the address on the back cover.

Illustration Credits: Enslow Publishers, Inc., pp. 19, 23, 25, 62;
Courtesy Los Alamos Historical Museum Photo Archives, pp. 37, 43,
45, 46, 52, 71, 73, 74, 77; National Archives, pp. 14, 28, 31, 35, 40, 50,
56, 60, 79, 91, 93, 94, 105, 107, 113; Reproduced from the *Dictionary of
American Portraits*, Published by Dover Publications, Inc., in 1967, p. 8.

Cover Illustration: National Archives; Courtesy Los Alamos Historical
Museum Photo Archives.

★ Contents ★

MISSION: POSSIBLE

Imagine keeping a secret among a hundred thousand people. Or hiding three whole cities. Envision gathering several of the most famous scientists in the world in one place for three years without anyone knowing where they were or what they were doing. Picture midnight escapes in small boats across icy oceans, or living next door to a fun-loving baby-sitter who was really a Russian spy. Imagine the vice president of the United States not knowing that people all across America were working day and night to build a new kind of weapon. Then imagine this weapon changing the course of history. This scenario reads like a movie script with an unbelievable plot. But it is not. These things really happened during the 1940s when the United States was working to develop the atomic bomb.

President Franklin Delano Roosevelt ordered the army to build the bomb in 1942. At that time, scientists did not yet know whether such a weapon was even possible. Most speculated that, if it were, its development would take years. Thousands of complex mathematical calculations had to be made, and hundreds of questions

President Franklin Roosevelt ordered the construction of the first atomic bomb.

still needed answers. And even if an atomic bomb were possible, making enough fuel for one might not be. This alone was such an immense manufacturing task that, as one scientist put it, the entire nation would have to be "turned into a factory."[1]

Military leaders saw another obstacle—secrecy. The world was engaged in World War II, and enemies of the United States were also working on atomic bombs. The country that built one first would probably win the war. This race made the smallest leak of information dangerous. Creating a nuclear weapon would require the help of thousands of people across the United States. In addition, the project would take years to complete. Could this many people keep a secret for this long?

The scientists who worked on the first atomic bomb knew they could change the course of history. In fact, many hoped to do just that. Their work brought science and politics together as had never been done before. However, the creation of the atomic weapon is more than just a lesson in history. It is one of the most fascinating stories of our time.

2

DISCOVERY!

The atomic bomb had its roots in politics as much as in science. During the 1930s, Adolf Hitler rose to power as the chancellor of Germany. He was the leader of the National Socialist German Workers' political party, or Nazi party for short.

Hitler and the Nazi Party

The Nazis were angry that Germany had been divided into several small countries after losing World War I. They wanted to reunite these countries into one nation made up of people they called Aryans. The Nazis defined Aryans as a race of people native to western Europe. They believed Aryans were the only true Germans and were the best people in the world, the earth's "supreme race." The Nazis considered people of other backgrounds inferior and undesirable. They especially hated people of Jewish or Slavic heritage.

Hitler knew that many Germans would not agree with these racist ideas, so he said little about them to the general public. Instead, he talked about building a stronger nation and a healthy economy. These ideas appealed to Germans. After World War I, Germany was forced to pay huge sums of money to the countries that won as a punishment for having started the war. By the 1930s, the German economy was in a depression, and millions of Germans were unemployed. Their desperate predicament made Hitler popular, and in 1933 he became Germany's chancellor (chief minister of the nation).

For Hitler, this position was a stepping-stone to complete control. As chancellor, he had a lot of power, which he used whenever possible to get rid of government leaders who did not agree with his ideas. By the middle of 1934, Hitler had achieved a position of ultimate power. He was now Germany's dictator.

As Germany's sole ruler, Hitler began taking away freedoms. He forbade the country's newspapers and radio stations to express opinions he did not like. He declared that all political parties were illegal—except for the Nazi party. All German teenagers were forced to join junior military clubs in which they were taught Nazi beliefs. Children were told to spy on their parents and report any anti-Nazi talk they heard. When they did, their parents were often arrested.

Then Hitler began making laws against non-Aryans. His first law said that only Aryans could be public employees. Consequently, about ten thousand teachers, professors, and scientists were fired. Many were Jewish. Thousands of them left the country. Some moved to nearby countries, where they hoped they would be safe from Hitler's racism. Others traveled to Great Britain or to the United States.

Germany lost about one fourth of its physicists as a result.

Hitler eventually enacted four hundred laws that discriminated against non-Aryans. One law forbid Aryans to marry Jews. Another said that Jewish people could no longer be German citizens. These new laws were enforced by German police called the Gestapo. The Gestapo jailed or killed anyone who disobeyed the Nazis. After each law was enacted, more Jews left Germany. When they did, the German government made it difficult for them to return.

Among the many Jews who fled Germany was famous scientist Albert Einstein. Einstein had been born in Germany in 1879. By 1905, he had earned a worldwide reputation as a brilliant physicist. He had been awarded the Nobel Prize in physics—one of the most prestigious awards in the world—in 1921. Still, Hitler branded Einstein as inferior because he was Jewish.

When Einstein visited the United States in 1933, the German government seized his property and took away his citizenship. But Einstein did not want to return to Germany. He believed the Nazis were turning Germany into a sick, destructive country.[1]

Hitler's actions aroused concern outside Germany, too. People in nearby countries worried about the spread of anti-Semitism, or the hatred of Jewish people. Among those concerned was a famed Italian physicist named Enrico Fermi, whose wife was Jewish. Fermi feared that Italy's ruler, Benito Mussolini, might

THE NUREMBERG LAWS ON CITIZENSHIP AND RACE, 1935

FIRST SUPPLEMENTARY DECREE OF NOVEMBER 14, 1935:

ARTICLE 4. (1) A JEW CANNOT BE A CITIZEN OF THE REICH. HE CANNOT EXERCISE THE RIGHT TO VOTE; HE CANNOT OCCUPY PUBLIC OFFICE. . . .

ARTICLE 5. (1) A JEW IS AN INDIVIDUAL WHO IS DESCENDED FROM AT LEAST THREE GRANDPARENTS WHO WERE, RACIALLY, FULL JEWS. . . .

THE LAW FOR THE PROTECTION OF GERMAN BLOOD AND HONOR, SEPTEMBER 15, 1935:

ARTICLE 1. (1) ANY MARRIAGES BETWEEN JEWS AND CITIZENS OF GERMAN OR KINDRED BLOOD ARE HEREWITH FORBIDDEN. MARRIAGES ENTERED INTO DESPITE THIS LAW ARE INVALID, EVEN IF THEY ARE ARRANGED ABROAD AS A MEANS OF CIRCUMVENTING THIS LAW. . . .

ARTICLE 2. EXTRAMARITAL RELATIONS BETWEEN JEWS AND CITIZENS OF GERMAN OR KINDRED BLOOD ARE HEREWITH FORBIDDEN.

ARTICLE 3. JEWS ARE FORBIDDEN TO EMPLOY AS SERVANTS IN THEIR HOUSEHOLDS FEMALE SUBJECTS OF GERMAN OR KINDRED BLOOD WHO ARE UNDER THE AGE OF 45 YEARS.[2]

When Adolf Hitler came to power in Germany, he began to pass laws that severely restricted the freedom of Jewish people.

adopt Hitler's racist attitudes and laws. But Fermi tried to ignore politics by concentrating on his scientific studies.

Investigating Atoms

At the time, Fermi was studying atoms, the tiny particles that make up everything on the earth. There are many different kinds of atoms. A substance made of only one kind of atom is called an element. For example, hydrogen is an element made of only hydrogen atoms. Sometimes two or more elements combine to form new substances. These are called compounds. Water, for instance, is a compound made when two hydrogen atoms combine with one oxygen atom. Atoms are too small to be seen by the human eye. It takes more than a million atoms lined up next to each

Italian physicist Enrico Fermi was instrumental in unlocking the secrets of atomic power.

other to make a string as wide as a human hair. But atoms are not the smallest pieces of matter. Atoms are made from smaller particles called protons, neutrons, and electrons. Protons and neutrons cling together in the center of an atom, or nucleus. Electrons whirl around the nucleus at high speeds.

During 1934, Fermi was studying atoms by shooting neutrons into the nuclei of various kinds of atoms. He was particularly intrigued by the behavior of uranium nuclei. When he shot neutrons into them, Fermi could tell that the atoms changed. But Fermi could not figure out what the atoms were doing. He did not realize that he had actually split the uranium atom. He reported his observations to other scientists. Many of them began duplicating Fermi's experiment, hoping they could find out what was happening. One of these scientists was Lise Meitner, an Austrian physicist who worked with German scientists Otto Hahn and Fritz Strassman.

Hitler Invades Europe

At about this time, Fermi's political fears began coming true. In 1935, Italy's Mussolini and Germany's Hitler became allies, agreeing to help each other in conflicts with other nations. Germany and Italy became known as the Axis Powers. When Mussolini began making anti-Semitic laws in Italy, Fermi and his wife discussed leaving their homeland.

So did other European Jews. Hitler took over Austria in March 1938. He immediately declared that all Austrian citizens were subject to German law. Now Austrian Jews, including Lise Meitner, fled the Nazis. Meitner joined her physicist nephew, Otto Frisch, in Denmark. He was working with another famous physicist, Niels Bohr. Meitner told them about her work with the German physicists. It was not long before she received a letter from her German colleagues, telling her more about their experiments.

Hahn and Strassman had solved part of the mystery of the changing uranium atoms. They had found that when a uranium nucleus was struck by a neutron, the nucleus split into two almost-equal parts. Their discovery led to yet another question. When Hahn and Strassman weighed these two parts, they found that their combined weight was a little less than the total weight of the previously whole nucleus. What had happened to the missing weight?

As Hahn and Strassman thought about this, Hitler ordered a brutal assault against Jewish people, which would become known as *Kristallnacht*, or the "Night of Broken Glass." The attack began on November 9, 1938. For two days, the Nazis attacked and destroyed the homes, businesses, and synagogues of all known Jews. They killed anyone who resisted. During these forty-eight hours, over thirty-five thousand Jews were arrested. They were sent to concentration camps.

Concentration camps had originally been built to imprison people who disagreed with Nazi ideas. Now they became prisons for Jewish people. The camps were crowded and dirty, and the guards there were cruel. By the autumn of 1938, the German government was holding sixty thousand people in three main concentration camps.

The United States, Great Britain, and France condemned Hitler's actions, but none of the countries wanted to take military action against him. He continued his plan to expand German territory unopposed. In September 1938, Hitler moved his army into Czechoslovakia.

Fermi Wins the Nobel Prize

By now, the Fermis were desperate to leave Italy.[3] But they knew the anti-Semitic government might not let them go. They found a solution when Enrico Fermi was awarded the 1938 Nobel Prize in physics. Fermi was honored, but more important, it gave him a chance to leave Italy. Fermi hoped the Italian authorities would let him travel to Sweden to accept the award. If they did, he would ask them to let his family come along. From Sweden, they would travel to New York City, where Fermi had been invited to teach at Columbia University. Although the guest position was only supposed to last seven months, the Fermis secretly planned to stay much longer. They were careful not to tip off Italian authorities to that fact, however. They packed just a few bags and gave only their closest friends a real good-bye. As they climbed aboard the train that would start their journey, they worried about being stopped. They were not.

On December 10, 1938, Enrico Fermi stepped onto a stage in Sweden to accept his award. He spent the next several days in nearby Denmark. While he was there, he talked with Niels Bohr about current atomic research. Then on December 24, Fermi and his family boarded a ship bound for the United States. By the start of the new year, they were in New York City.

The Discovery of Fission

When Bohr made a trip to the United States that January, he visited Fermi to tell him about a fascinating theory presented by the two Austrian physicists working in his laboratory, Lise Meitner and Otto Frisch. Meitner and Frisch believed they had solved the puzzle of the uranium nuclei's missing weight. They said that the lost weight proved Albert Einstein's famous theory that matter could be changed into energy. Einstein had described this idea in a formula: $E=mc^2$. The E stands for energy, the m represents an object's mass, and c is the speed of light. According to Meitner and Frisch, the weight loss was the amount of mass that had been transformed into energy. They named the splitting of the uranium atom "fission."

Fermi immediately understood what this meant. If enough atoms could be split and their energy captured, a tremendous new source of energy would be created. By the end of January, physicists all over the world had heard about fission. Several were already brainstorming ways its energy might be used. Given the

Fission

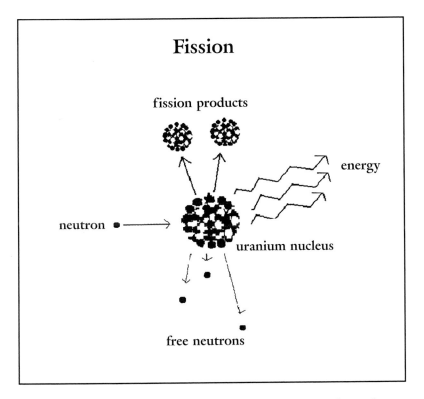

When a free neutron hits a uranium atom's nucleus, the nucleus is split into pieces, releasing energy as well as several neutrons and protons. Most of these subatomic particles regroup to form the nuclei of a different element. But a few neutrons fly off randomly with enough force to split the nucleus of other uranium atoms.

conditions in Europe, some scientists were thinking about one use in particular—weaponry. Fermi believed that a bomb made from atomic energy could be incredibly powerful. "A little bomb like that," Fermi told a friend while cupping his hands, "and it would all disappear."[4]

3

ALERT!

Before long, scientists were calculating the potential power of a nuclear weapon, one created by the splitting of the atom. Most estimated that a bomb made from one pound of uranium might be as destructive as one made from eight thousand tons of TNT, one of the most powerful explosives known. However, these were only equations on a chalkboard. Designing and building a real bomb would require years of study and experimentation.

Informing President Roosevelt

At the time, the only known element that fissioned was uranium, and it was scarce. It became even more scarce in the summer of 1939 when Hitler banned its export from Czechoslovakian mines. Most of the American public did not see this ban as important. But Enrico Fermi and a few other physicists immediately grasped its significance—German scientists must be thinking about atomic weapons.

Now Fermi imagined something even more frightening than Hitler's rise to power: Hitler with an atomic bomb. Two of Fermi's colleagues, Leo Szilard and Eugene Wigner, shared his horror. Both had been born in Hungary, were Jewish, and had left Europe because of anti-Semitism. All three men agreed that they must alert United States President Franklin Roosevelt.

Wigner and Szilard wrote a letter outlining the issue. They explained that "uranium may be turned into a new and important source of energy in the immediate future." They went on to say that this energy might be used for "the construction of bombs . . . extremely powerful bombs."[1] In August 1939, they took their letter to the scientist they believed could influence Roosevelt—Albert Einstein. Einstein agreed to help. He signed his name to the letter, then gave it

SOURCE DOCUMENT

SOME RECENT WORK BY E. FERMI AND L. SZILARD, WHICH HAS BEEN COMMUNICATED TO ME IN MANUSCRIPT, LEADS ME TO EXPECT THAT THE ELEMENT URANIUM MAY BE TURNED INTO A NEW AND IMPORTANT SOURCE OF ENERGY IN THE IMMEDIATE FUTURE. . . . THIS NEW PHENOMENON WOULD ALSO LEAD TO THE CONSTRUCTION OF BOMBS, AND IT IS CONCEIVABLE—THOUGH MUCH LESS CERTAIN—THAT EXTREMELY POWERFUL BOMBS OF A NEW TYPE MAY THUS BE CONSTRUCTED. A SINGLE BOMB OF THIS TYPE, CARRIED BY BOAT AND EXPLODED IN A PORT, MIGHT VERY WELL DESTROY THE WHOLE PORT TOGETHER WITH SOME OF THE SURROUNDING TERRITORY. . . .[2]

Albert Einstein wrote this letter to President Roosevelt, detailing the findings of Fermi and Szilard, and warning him of the possibility that Germany was working to develop an atomic bomb.

to a friend of President Roosevelt's, Alexander Sachs.[3] Sachs promised to deliver the letter to the president personally.

Great Britain and France Declare War

On September 1, 1939, the German Army invaded Poland. Great Britain and France watched, hoping the Soviet Union would come to Poland's aid. The leader of the Soviet Union, Joseph Stalin, however, had already made a secret pact with Hitler. Stalin had agreed not to oppose Hitler in exchange for half of a conquered Poland.

It now seemed clear that Hitler intended to take over as much of Europe as he could. This meant that Great Britain and France were in danger of invasion. These countries' leaders had to act. On September 3, 1939, they declared war on Germany, and became known as the Allies.

Soon, Alexander Sachs was sitting in President Roosevelt's office, reading him the scientists' letter. It was filled with words and ideas that neither Sachs nor Roosevelt understood. But both knew they were reading information that was extremely important. Roosevelt passed the letter to his top military advisor, telling him, "this requires action."[4] Before long, Roosevelt authorized the formation of a special group called the Advisory Committee on Uranium to look into the matter. This committee was told to determine whether atomic weapons were really possible.

After Germany invaded Poland in 1939, Great Britain and France declared war. Other European nations soon followed, dividing Europe between the Allies and the Axis Powers.

Splitting the Atom

While they met, Fermi was thinking about how to split enough uranium atoms to create a useful amount of energy. The biggest problem he saw was finding a source of neutrons for the work. His present equipment was only capable of bombarding a few neutrons at a few atoms. Billions of atoms would have to be split to create any useful amount of energy.

Fermi pondered the chain-reaction theory that some scientists had proposed. They knew that when a neutron hit a uranium atom's nucleus, the nucleus broke apart. Two parts of the split nuclei immediately formed atoms of another element. But a few of the neutrons flew out of the nucleus without joining others. If these ejected neutrons hit the nuclei of other uranium atoms, they would probably split them. When this happened, more neutrons would be released to strike more nuclei. The splitting, therefore, would create a chain reaction of continually splitting nuclei. With enough uranium, this constant atom-splitting would create plenty of energy. In fact, with the right amount of uranium, the self-sustaining chain reaction would become so fast, it would result in an explosion. Therefore, if the chain-reaction theory proved true, the neutrons needed to create atomic energy could come from the uranium itself.

Hitler Marches On

Fermi contemplated this possibility as Germany marched on. In early April 1940, Hitler entered

Chain Reaction

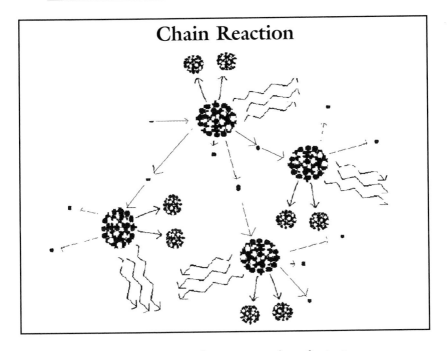

A chain reaction occurs when neutrons from fissioning atoms split other atoms. This splitting releases energy and more nuclei-splitting neutrons. If enough neutrons begin the action, the splitting will continue on its own. This is called a self-sustaining chain reaction.

Norway and Denmark. Niels Bohr watched, knowing that if the Germans broke into his lab, they might seize information that would help them make their own nuclear weapon. Therefore, he hid his most important documents and substances, including some water that contained a special kind of hydrogen. This rare "heavy water" was extremely useful in Bohr's atomic experiments. Bohr poured the valuable liquid into a beer bottle and put it in his laboratory refrigerator next to real beer. He hoped that if his laboratory were raided, the Germans would not search his refrigerator.[5]

By the end of May, Germany had conquered the Netherlands and Belgium. This time it was the foresight of M. Edgar Sengier, a Belgian businessman, that would prove vital to the Allies' efforts. At the time, Belgium controlled the African country Belgian Congo, where one of the world's largest deposits of uranium was located. Sengier was the director of the company that mined this uranium. Having recently been told by an English scientist that his mine's uranium might be important for a new kind of weapon, Sengier promptly ordered his mines to ship all available uranium to New York City when the Germans invaded Belgium. Over 1,250 tons of uranium ore were sent to a warehouse on Staten Island. These crates of ore would sit in storage for the next few years.[6]

On June 14, German tanks rolled into Paris and took over the French government. Then Hitler began bombing air-force bases in Great Britain. England's prime minister, Winston Churchill, was determined to fight back. He pledged that England would "fight on the beaches . . . fight on the landing-grounds . . . fight in the fields and in the streets . . . [and] never surrender."[7] Meanwhile, Mussolini pushed farther into Africa, invading British Somaliland and Egypt.

The war in Europe divided United States public opinion. Some Americans wanted the nation to stay out of the war completely. Others thought the United States should help the nations that were being invaded. President Roosevelt followed a path of compromise. He provided the Allies with weapons and other necessities, but did not send United States troops into the war.

Japan Joins Germany

As time passed, however, this position became more difficult to maintain, because another country was becoming increasingly aggressive. During the 1930s, Japan had taken over Manchuria, eastern China, and parts of Indochina. Now Japanese leaders spoke of controlling all of Southeast Asia. In September 1940, Japan joined the alliance between Italy and Germany. But the Allies had few resources to use to keep the Japanese out of Asia. Their attention and forces were concentrated on fighting the Nazis in Europe. Still, America watched from the sidelines.

Lawrence and Oppenheimer

In the meantime, two American scientists, Ernest O. Lawrence and J. Robert Oppenheimer, were studying fission at the University of California. Lawrence had invented a machine called a cyclotron that helped him experiment with uranium atoms. Oppenheimer thought about how these atoms could be used to create an enormously destructive weapon.

Oppenheimer had been born to Jewish parents in 1904 in New York City. During the 1920s, he had attended Harvard University, then traveled to Germany to study physics. He received a doctorate there in 1927, then left Germany just before Hitler rose to power. When Oppenheimer returned to the United States, he bought a vacation cabin in New

American scientist Dr. J. Robert Oppenheimer studied physics in Germany before accepting a position at the University of California. He helped build the physics department there into one of the best in the nation.

Mexico, where he took long horseback rides around Santa Fe. Then he went to work at the University of California, helping to make its physics department one of the best in the nation.

While Lawrence and Oppenheimer studied uranium, other scientists at the California lab looked for more elements that might fission. Four scientists there—Glenn Seaborg, Edwin M. McMillan, Joseph W. Kennedy, and Arthur C. Wahl—soon discovered another element that fissioned: plutonium. Although plutonium was even more rare than uranium, the physicists learned to make it from uranium.

Hitler's "Final Solution"

As scientists all over the world studied fission, Adolf Hitler stormed into Greece and Yugoslavia. In June 1941, he broke his treaty with Soviet leader Joseph Stalin and invaded the Soviet Union. The Soviets responded by joining the Allies. But this did not stop Hitler. He secretly moved ahead with what he called his "final solution" to the "Jewish problem."

Hitler's "final solution" was genocide—the extermination of a group of people. He planned to murder every Jewish person he could. Hitler began with the Jews in conquered areas of the Soviet Union. Thousands were ruthlessly shot, forced into buildings that were then set on fire, or driven into the sea to drown. Hitler kept these massacres secret from the world.

Another huge secret was about to be revealed, and it would change the course of the war.

4

★ ★ ★
★ ★
★ ★
★ ★
★ ★ ★

ONE THEORY PROVEN

On the morning of December 7, 1941, 360 Japanese war planes took off from aircraft carriers floating 230 miles from the Hawaiian Islands. The planes were headed for Pearl Harbor, a naval base on Oahu, Hawaii. Pearl Harbor was the headquarters for the United States Pacific Fleet, the ships used for conflicts in the Pacific Ocean. Japanese leaders wanted to destroy the fleet, believing it was the only force strong enough to stop their plans for taking over Southeast Asia.

Attack on Pearl Harbor

At 7:55 A.M., the Japanese planes suddenly appeared over Pearl Harbor, and the base was caught by surprise. Consequently, it was unprepared to fight back. In less than two hours, Japanese bombs destroyed almost two hundred United States planes and sank five huge American battleships. One, the *Arizona*, went down with over a thousand men trapped inside. By the time the attack ended, over two thousand Americans had been killed. The United States Pacific Fleet had been crippled.

The Japanese attack on Pearl Harbor in 1941 caught the United States naval base there by complete surprise.

America's response was swift. On December 8, the United States declared war on Japan. Canada and Great Britain soon followed suit. Then China declared war on the Axis Powers, and Germany and Italy declared war on the United States. Other countries joined in the fight, and as 1942 began, thirty nations had sided with the Allies while nine made up the Axis Powers.

The world was again at war.

SOURCE DOCUMENT

YESTERDAY, DECEMBER 7, 1941—A DATE WHICH WILL LIVE IN INFAMY—THE UNITED STATES OF AMERICA WAS SUDDENLY AND DELIBERATELY ATTACKED BY NAVAL AND AIR FORCES OF THE EMPIRE OF JAPAN.

THE UNITED STATES WAS AT PEACE WITH THAT NATION AND, AT THE SOLICITATION OF JAPAN, WAS STILL IN CONVERSATION WITH ITS GOVERNMENT AND ITS EMPEROR LOOKING TOWARD THE MAINTENANCE OF PEACE IN THE PACIFIC. . . .

THE ATTACK YESTERDAY ON THE HAWAIIAN ISLANDS HAS CAUSED SEVERE DAMAGE TO AMERICAN NAVAL AND MILITARY FORCES. I REGRET TO TELL YOU THAT VERY MANY AMERICAN LIVES HAVE BEEN LOST. . . .

I ASK THAT CONGRESS DECLARE THAT SINCE THE UNPROVOKED AND DASTARDLY ATTACK BY JAPAN ON SUNDAY, DECEMBER 7, 1941, A STATE OF WAR HAS EXISTED BETWEEN THE UNITED STATES AND JAPAN.[1]

After Japan attacked Pearl Harbor, President Roosevelt asked Congress to declare war.

Roosevelt Orders an Atomic Bomb

In June 1942, the Advisory Committee on Uranium reported to President Roosevelt that a nuclear weapon might be made "in time to influence the outcome of the present war."[2] He immediately ordered the army to build one.

This job was given to the Army Corps of Engineers, the division of the army that directs engineering tasks. The Corps of Engineers was divided into small groups called districts, and each one handled a specific project. On June 18, 1942, Colonel J. C. Marshall was told to set up a new district for a top secret assignment. Because Marshall's office was in New York City, the new district was named the Manhattan District. Official papers listed the purpose of the Manhattan District as the "development of substitute materials."[3] At the time, most people had no idea what this meant. Only a few knew that the Manhattan District was going to make an atomic bomb. This mission became known as the Manhattan Project.

One of Marshall's highest priorities was keeping the project a secret. Any information, no matter how insignificant it might seem, could be the information that helped the Germans build the bomb first. This meant that the open discussion going on between scientists in different parts of the country had to be stopped. Marshall immediately opened a central laboratory where the top nuclear physicists could work. Located on the campus of the University of Chicago, it was called the Metallurgical Laboratory. This name might help keep the real purpose of the lab unknown. Hopefully, the general public would assume that its purpose was researching ordinary metals. By the fall of 1942, more than a thousand scientists were working at the "Met Lab." Among them were Fermi, Szilard, and Wigner. But even a thousand scientists were not enough. Many others, including Lawrence and Oppenheimer, still worked on aspects of the project in other locations around the country.

It was soon clear that the biggest obstacle would be making enough fuel. Uranium and plutonium were the only known possibilities, and both were scarce. This difficulty was magnified by the fact that a nuclear bomb needed a special kind of uranium called U-235, a form that was present in less than one percent of the more common uranium, U-238. As some scientists developed ways to separate the two, others experimented with various plutonium-making processes.

Groves Takes Over the Manhattan Project

On September 23, 1942, Brigadier General Leslie R. Groves replaced Colonel Marshall as the leader of the Manhattan Project. Groves had just finished directing the building of the Pentagon. This huge new building would be the headquarters of the United States Department of Defense. Groves's first task with the Manhattan Project was finding a place to build a factory for separating uranium, even though the scientists still were not sure how it would be done. He selected

General Leslie R. Groves was put in charge of the Manhattan Project in September 1942.

a site about twenty miles from Knoxville, Tennessee, in an area known as Black Oak Ridge. Few people lived in the area. The isolation would help maintain secrecy. He hired the Stone and Webster Engineering Company to build the factory and another company called Tennessee Eastman to operate it. The code name for the plant was Site X.

Next, Groves turned his attention to finding a central location for the handful of scientists he predicted would be needed to design a bomb. This might well be the most secret part of the entire project. Groves wanted a place that was remote. Any roads leading to it must be easy to close and monitor. Insiders were asked if they knew of any such place, and Oppenheimer suggested an area near his vacation home in New Mexico. The Pajarito Plateau was sandwiched between mountains and the Rio Grande. Steep canyons cut through the plateau, dividing it into a series of high mesas.

Only a few hardy souls had ever lived on the Pajarito. The first permanent settlers were probably the Tewa Indians, who had lived there during the 1200s. They had farmed the mesas and lived in houses dug into the cliffs. The Tewa could spy marauders from their lofty homes before they were close enough to do any harm. During the 1600s, the Tewa moved down from the plateau and settled along the Rio Grande next to people who had come from other areas around the Southwest. These American Indians were all given the general name of Pueblo Indians. Some of their descendants still live in small towns along the Rio Grande today.

After the Tewa left the plateau, it remained uninhabited until American homesteaders appeared there in the early 1900s. In 1916, a man named Ashley Pond turned one of these homesteaded ranches into a private school for boys. He called it the Los Alamos Ranch School. Oppenheimer had been to the school on a few of his horseback rides. He told Groves that it might be a good place for the bomb-making lab.

Groves looked over the area and liked it. Few people would know about the closing of a small school in the mountains of New Mexico. The nearest town was Santa Fe, eighteen miles away. Only one winding dirt road led from Santa Fe to the mesa top. Like the Tewa Indians who had lived there centuries earlier, military

Before the United States government built a laboratory on the Los Alamos mesa, it was a private school for boys, part of which was located behind a field of crops.

personnel could see people approaching from miles around. Groves asked the army to buy the land as a demolition range. His request was approved.

Fermi's Chain Reaction

Back at the Met Lab in Chicago, Fermi was making plans to test the chain-reaction theory. He had designed a primitive nuclear reactor made from several layers of graphite blocks. These would be stacked into a globe twenty-six feet tall and twenty-six feet wide at the center. Each layer would contain several uranium nuggets for fissioning. As its atoms split, the graphite would slow the released neutrons. Slow-moving neutrons were known to split more nuclei than rapidly moving ones. Each layer had channels across it to hold cadmium-coated steel rods. Cadmium absorbs uranium nuclei, so the rods would be slid in and out as the reactor needed speeding up or slowing down.

The physicists believed they could create a self-sustaining chain reaction. They also felt they could stop one before it exploded. But they knew their reactor pile might become hot enough to liquefy the uranium or start a huge blaze. Furthermore, they were aware that anyone who was exposed to the reaction could be poisoned by radiation—the energy given off by fissioning atoms. Small amounts of radiation are not harmful, but large doses can damage living tissue. The scientists knew their pile would be radioactive, but they did not know how much radiation it would create. Nor did they know exactly what level was lethal.

With all of the unknowns, it seemed best to build the reactor in an isolated area. Then, if something went wrong, not many people would be hurt.

But time was of the essence. Hitler's army was strong. More frightening was the fear that German scientists were closer to creating an atomic weapon than the Allies were. So the original plan to build the reactor outside Chicago was changed. This would waste time, and there was no time to waste. The Met Lab physicists decided to build the pile in the most convenient place available—a racketball court under the stands of an old football stadium on the University of Chicago campus.

The building began on November 7, 1942. As each layer was set in place, the scientists measured how many loose neutrons were flying around inside it. The number steadily increased. By December 1, five hundred tons of graphite blocks surrounded fifty tons of uranium in forty-eight neatly stacked layers. By 4:00 P.M., their calculations indicated that the pile was nearing a self-sustained chain reaction. Excitement mounted. The scientists knew they were close to making a scientific discovery. But realizing that the chain reaction was still hours away, Fermi told everyone to go home.

A night crew stayed to add three more layers. By 9:30 the next morning, people were scurrying about, making last minute preparations. Three men carried liquid cadmium to the top of a platform over the pile. Their job was to pour the cadmium over the reactor if it got out of control. The scientists hoped the cadmium would absorb enough uranium nuclei to stop any catastrophes. Another scientist stood ready to release a huge rod of boron steel into the pile for the same purpose. As one last precaution, someone was stationed near the cadmium rods to reinsert them if necessary.

The rest of the scientists gathered on a balcony over the pile to record the information from their various instruments. Fermi ordered the cadmium rods to be pulled out one by one. The withdrawal of each rod made the speed of the clicking counters increase.

Fifteen years after Enrico Fermi's chain-reaction experiment, artist Gary Sheehan recreated the scene in this painting. No photographers had been allowed at the 1942 event.

Finally, the last rod was pulled from the graphite. Inside the pile, neutrons were bouncing from one atom to another, splitting them apart to free more neutrons. By 3:20 P.M., the neutron counters were producing one continuous click. Fermi studied his instruments, made a few calculations, then looked up with a smile. "The reaction is self-sustaining," he said.[4]

Congratulations flew and a bottle of wine was opened. The news was reported to Washington, D.C., in a coded message. "The Italian navigator has just landed in the New World," the waiting officials were told. "Everyone landed safe and happy."[5] The first man-made, self-sustaining nuclear chain reaction had been created.

Five days later, students at the Los Alamos Ranch School in New Mexico were told that their school was closing and that they must vacate the area as soon as possible. No one was told why.

5

X, Y, AND W

On January 1, 1943, the United States government opened the Los Alamos Laboratory. It was called Site Y. The new laboratory would have two commanders: General Leslie Groves would be in charge of the military aspects of the project, and J. Robert Oppenheimer would head up the scientific research.

Choosing a Site for a Plutonium Factory

Even as the new lab was opening, Groves was off purchasing another site. This one would house a factory for making plutonium. At the time, "all of the world's plutonium could still have been piled on a pinhead, with room to spare."[1] It was clear that if a bomb were to be fueled by plutonium, much more would have to be made—and fast. Groves persuaded the Du Pont Company to help design and build a plutonium-making facility.

The plutonium factory, Site W, would be built on the Columbia River near Hanford, Washington. This was another sparsely populated area of the United States, and the government soon informed the few families who lived nearby that they had to sell their homes and leave. Again, no one was told why.

Now Groves was overseeing construction at three sites: Oak Ridge, Los Alamos, and Hanford. In addition to the factories and laboratories needed at these places, housing had to be built for thousands of workers. And everything had to be finished as soon as possible.

The Lab on the Mesa

In fact, scientists were already arriving at Los Alamos. Robert Wilson and Edwin M. McMillan were among the first. Edward Teller, a physicist who had left Hungary in 1935, and Italian immigrant Emilio Segrè

The original road to the top of the mesa had to be improved to allow for an increase in traffic.

soon joined them. Hans Bethe, a refugee from Germany, arrived in April.

These first arrivals settled into a lodge that had once housed the school's teachers. Their quarters were jokingly called "bathtub row," because the newly built housing would contain no bathtubs, only showers. While the scientists went to work, construction workers pounded away on new buildings. Apartments and labs popped up at an amazing rate, and there seemed to be a constant need for more. Groves had originally planned for a community of about three hundred people. His estimate turned out to be extremely low.

It became apparent rather quickly that many more people would be vital to the project's success. First of all, a wide range of scientists from many different fields would be needed. Experts on metals, explosives, and chemicals were all necessary. So were technicians of all sorts. Members of the Women's Army Corps (WAC) were needed as secretaries and chauffeurs. In addition, American Indian men and women from the towns below worked at construction and domestic jobs on the mesa. All of these people quickly raised the population to fifteen hundred, and the project was just beginning.

Even so, it was not always easy to find people to work at Los Alamos. Many were already working on the Manhattan Project in other places. Furthermore, the conditions of employment were a bit unusual. The location and purpose of the job could not be revealed, so applicants had no idea where they were headed or what they would do once there. As the wife of one scientist put it, agreeing to work on the project "was akin to the pioneer women accompanying their husbands across uncharted plains westward, alert to dangers, resigned to the fact that they journeyed, for weal or woe, into the Unknown."[2]

The first stop on this journey was an office in downtown Santa Fe. There, the newcomers met Dorothy McKibbin, Los Alamos' official "Welcome Wagon." She soothed frayed nerves, then made arrangements to transport the newest employees up the mesa.

Dorothy McKibbin and J. Robert Oppenheimer at a Los Alamos party.

Top Secret

Although everyone who came to Los Alamos already knew that the project was top secret, some were surprised by the extent to which security invaded their privacy. All residents were assigned a number that would be their official "name" while they lived there. Driver's licenses, bank accounts, insurance policies, and even tax returns were issued to these numbers. The most famous people were given new names to conceal their identities. For instance, whenever Enrico Fermi came to Los Alamos, he was called Henry Farmer.

Guards checked each car that left or entered Los Alamos for the proper permits and identification.

Furthermore, the mesa top was surrounded by a high barbed-wire fence that was patrolled by armed guards. No one came in and no one went out of the gates without permission. People who did leave Los Alamos were not allowed to travel more than one hundred miles away. Anyone who accidentally ran into a friend while gone had to give a detailed description of the meeting upon returning. Letters leaving Los Alamos were read and phone conversations were monitored. No one could tell outsiders the names of the people working at Los Alamos. In fact, residents could not even mention their coworkers' occupations. The word *physicist* was forbidden, and all of the scientists were called "engineers." Security also made sure that residents did not accidentally reveal the Los Alamos location by naming nearby towns or describing the surrounding countryside. Letters coming to the mesa were mailed to a box number that was a code for Los Alamos: United States Army, P.O. Box 1663.

Other security measures were less intrusive. For example, the buildings on the mesa were all painted the same color as the pine trees that surrounded them. This helped camouflage the buildings from the air. And the streets of Los Alamos remained unnamed in case a spy did slip by the guards. This might slow down a trespasser's progress to a particular building.

In spite of all the efforts to maintain secrecy, though, Santa Fe residents knew something unusual was happening on the mesa. Bulldozers chugging up the old road and numerous military vehicles in the area aroused attention. So did the sudden appearance of strangers with European accents wandering about Santa Fe. Many soon connected Dorothy McKibbin to the mesa secret. In fact, McKibbin occasionally received a phone call from a resident saying, "Dorothy, there's a strange-looking man here and he's lost."[3] Inevitably, the man would be looking for her office. But Santa Fe residents soon realized that the mesa mystery was somehow linked to United States security and that they should not ask questions. Army officials even forbade the Santa Fe newspaper from reporting any information about the secret community. The newspaper's editor agreed to this restriction, believing it was in the national interest.

Bohr Escapes Denmark

As the population at Los Alamos grew, Allied soldiers were invading Italy. Mussolini's army surrendered in September 1943, and the Soviets were pushing the Germans out of Soviet territory. The Allies had been bombing German cities mercilessly. However, German factories kept making war weapons and the morale of the German people remained high.

Niels Bohr stayed in Denmark until late autumn. When he learned that the Germans were coming to arrest him, he hastily gathered his important work, including the special bottle of "beer" in his laboratory refrigerator. Then he and his family climbed into a small boat and crossed the North Sea to Sweden. Once there, Bohr discovered that he had grabbed the wrong bottle. Instead of heavy water, the bottle contained ordinary beer.[4] But his family was safe. Soon Bohr was flying to England, where his colleagues welcomed him. Once there, he was told about the British atomic weapons research. He also learned that scientists in the United States were trying to develop a nuclear bomb. By the end of 1943, Bohr was in Los Alamos, working on the project.

Building the Factories

In the meantime, construction crews were building a thousand homes and four factories at Oak Ridge, Tennessee. The largest of these was shaped like a U, with each wing stretching out for half a mile. This uranium-separating factory covered forty-four square acres of land, and contained miles of pipes and thousands of pumps. It was so big it required its own specially built power plant, a complex large enough to light the city of Boston.

Once the Oak Ridge operation was under way, Groves turned his attention to Hanford, Washington. The area was largely uninhabited, so a hundred job recruiters were employed to hire some of the forty-five thousand workers who would be needed. But the recruiters had little knowledge of the project for which they were hiring people. They were simply given a list of needs—two hundred carpenters, twenty-five truck drivers, eighteen telephone operators—and told to find as many of the appropriate employees as possible. The

*It took an entire day for this factory at Oak Ridge,
Tennessee, to separate a few grams of U-235 from U-238.*

recruiters were sent to every state but two—Tennessee and New Mexico. Officials did not want anyone who had been in contact with the secret operations in those places to come to Hanford. There was always the slight chance that he or she would connect the two operations and figure out what was going on.

A Spy on the Mesa

Even more people were invited into the project. Twenty-one scientists who had been conducting nuclear research in Great Britain arrived at Los Alamos in December 1943. These men were topnotch scientists. Their leader was James Chadwick, the man who had discovered the neutron in 1932. Otto Frisch, Lise Meitner's nephew, was part of the team, too.

Another team member, Klaus Fuchs, would become known around Los Alamos as a quiet and hardworking man. Fuchs had been born in Germany but had fled from the Nazis in 1933. He eventually moved to England, where he earned a reputation as a fine physicist. He was well respected at Los Alamos. Fuchs liked children, so many parents frequently asked him to baby-sit. No one who knew Fuchs then would have guessed that he was actually a Soviet spy. But in 1950, he would admit to having passed scientific information to the Soviet Union during his time in the United States. Fuchs would then be sentenced to fourteen years in prison for his actions.[5]

The Race Against Germany

By the end of the year, Los Alamos was a bustling town. Rows of apartment buildings, barracks, and trailers lined dusty streets. Quonset huts were also built for the residents. These huts were long, narrow structures with semicircular roofs made from sheets of steel. They were fast to construct, an important asset at Los Alamos, where there never seemed to be enough housing.

Los Alamos was always growing, and this created many inconveniences. But the importance of the task before the scientists overshadowed every annoyance.

So many people were needed at the various Manhattan Project sites that housing shortages were common. Hundreds of families lived in hastily constructed modular homes or army Quonset huts.

Everyone at Los Alamos knew they were involved in an extraordinary mission. They were working on the cutting edge of science with an unlimited budget. They had access to any equipment they wanted. If a tool they needed did not exist, a factory somewhere in America stood ready to make it.

Furthermore, every scientist felt the pressure of the race with Germany. Many believed that the country that made the first atomic bomb would win the war. Oppenheimer once remarked, "Almost everyone knew that this job, if it were achieved, would be part of history. This sense of excitement, of devotion and of patriotism in the end prevailed."[6]

The scientists also understood that their successful work could have destructive capabilities beyond any previously imagined. They were creating the means by which thousands, perhaps millions, of people would be killed. For many of the workers at Los Alamos, this presented a huge moral dilemma: Was it right to end Hitler's reign of terror with a horrible new weapon?

Most scientists answered this question by reasoning that it was the better of two terrible choices.[7] They hoped that their work would ultimately save more lives than it destroyed. Many of the scientists working on the project came from the very countries Hitler had invaded. Several had lost loved ones to the Nazis. Most had families or friends living in a Nazi-occupied country. For them, the Manhattan Project was not just a mission of United States national interest. It was a personal mission as well.

6

INSIDE AN ATOMIC BOMB

As 1944 began, the United States military was pushing Japan off several of the Pacific islands it had invaded. The "army" working on the atomic bomb was pushing on, too. The three major construction sites were progressing well. People were also working on the project in several other places.

The Secret Army

At Columbia University in New York City, scientists were devising better ways for the factories at Oak Ridge and Hanford to separate uranium or make plutonium. The Allis-Chalmers Company in Milwaukee, Wisconsin, built pumps for the plants. A company in Decatur, Illinois, made other special equipment. Researchers on the campus of Iowa State University developed ways to make U-238 more usable while Colorado miners pulled more of it out of the ground. And warehouse workers on Staten Island loaded uranium ore that had come from an African mine onto trucks bound for unknown destinations.

However, few of the people at any of these places knew they were helping to make an atomic weapon.

Nor did they know that there were others working toward the same goal. Each person knew only one thing: how to perform his or her particular job.

For example, hundreds of women at Oak Ridge did nothing more than sit on a stool all day, watching gauges. When a needle moved outside a specified limit, they were to adjust their knobs until the needle settled back into the correct range. These women had no idea that their adjustments were helping to extract U-235 from U-238. Even if they had known, they probably would not have understood why they were doing it. In fact, most of the physicists at Oak Ridge did not know that their work was connected to an atomic weapon. One later said that even if he had wanted to divulge vital information to an enemy spy, he would not have known what to say.[1]

Particularly baffling was the fact that although Oak Ridge workers saw huge amounts of a waxy white material (a form of uranium) going into the plant, no one ever saw a product leaving. This was because the final product of the huge factory amounted to only a few grams of material a day. Once or twice a week, government agents dressed in street clothes and carrying concealed weapons came to Oak Ridge to collect the U-235. They put it in a briefcase, then drove to Knoxville. At Knoxville, they boarded a train bound for Chicago. In Chicago, they passed the briefcase to different agents, who took it to Santa Fe by railroad. This process would be repeated week after week and

Most Manhattan Project employees had no idea they were helping to make an atomic bomb. These women at Oak Ridge, Tennessee, knew only how to perform a specific job.

month after month until the amount of U-235 at Los Alamos grew to several pounds.

Yet in spite of the workers' lack of knowledge about the Manhattan Project, Oak Ridge employees were repeatedly warned not to talk about their jobs with anyone outside the plant. Doing so carried the threat of a $10,000 fine and ten years in jail. Authorities told the workers that when someone asked what they were making, they were to say, "I'm making $1.35 an hour."[2] All the secrecy was part of Leslie Groves's security strategy called compartmentalization. Compartmentalization keeps each person in a large operation unaware of the finished product. This makes each worker like one tiny piece of a jigsaw puzzle. None of the individual pieces knows about the other pieces, so no one ever sees what the whole picture looks like.

Groves used compartmentalization in every aspect of the Manhattan Project except one: the labs at Los Alamos. Actually, Groves tried to compartmentalize there, too. He had originally wanted each lab to keep its work secret from the others. But Oppenheimer objected.[3] He told Groves that the discoveries made by some scientists might help others. Just as important, the work in one lab often affected the work of another.

For example, some scientists were busy calculating how much uranium was needed to create a chain reaction that would make a bomb explode. This amount is called the critical mass, and it was crucial that scientists figured it exactly right. If the bomb were made without enough fuel, it would fizzle. If it had too much material, the explosion might occur too soon.

While these scientists calculated, men in another lab designed a metal envelope that would surround the uranium. This envelope would bounce loose neutrons back into the uranium to help keep the chain reaction alive. But the number of neutrons that bounced back depended on the shape of the envelope and the material from which it was made. Therefore, the size of the critical mass depended on the design of the metal envelope. If all of these scientists did not communicate with each other, serious errors could be made.

Issues like these convinced Groves of the need for open communication among the scientists at Los Alamos. So every week they gathered to discuss their progress and problems. They also talked shop while eating, hiking, or socializing. Indeed, physics seemed to dominate every conversation on the mesa.

A Community of Geniuses

After sitting in on one of the scientific discussions, Groves told a friend, ". . . we [have] gathered on this mesa the largest collection of crackpots ever seen."[4] But the "crackpots" were brilliant. The mesa lab was populated with the greatest scientific minds of the time. Some had already won a Nobel Prize. Many more would.

The scientists were young, too. Their average age was twenty-nine. Most came to the mesa with children, and sometimes it seemed that babies were everywhere. Oppenheimer himself had an infant daughter and a toddler son. Consequently, a school was needed, and it was not long before Los Alamos had one for students from first through twelfth grade. In addition, there was a town council, a daycare center, and several recreational organizations.

But for the scientists, there was little time for play. They worked frantically from dawn to dark seven days a week. Still, they sometimes felt as if they were not making progress quickly enough.[5] But by the spring of 1944, the scientists had designed two different kinds of bombs. Both would have a nuclear core the size of a baseball. One core would be made of U-235. The other bomb's core would be of plutonium.

"Little Boy" and "Fat Man"

The two bombs would work differently. The first one was approximately ten feet long and two feet tall. Inside, a long metal barrel stretched between a uranium core and a uranium bullet. A powerful explosive rested behind the bullet. When it was detonated, the bullet would be fired into the uranium core, adding just enough U-235 to create a critical mass. This would set off a chain reaction that would create an explosion. This bomb became known as "Little Boy."

The second design was called an implosion device. It was oval-shaped and about eleven feet long and five feet tall. Inside it, a sphere of small explosives surrounded a ball of plutonium. When these explosives were set

The uranium-triggered bomb was nicknamed "Little Boy" because of its sleek shape.

off, they would squeeze the plutonium together. At a certain point, the compression would create a critical mass of plutonium and start a chain reaction that would explode. This bomb was nicknamed "Fat Man."

Fat Man was a much more complicated bomb than Little Boy. In order for it to work, the conventional explosions all had to occur at a precise time. This kind of precision required the development of sophisticated detonation devices. Scientists knew that Little Boy would explode. But because Fat Man was so complex, they wanted to test it.

This brought up a new problem. Plutonium was still precious. If Fat Man failed, the little plutonium that existed would be wasted. It could be months before more was ready. During those months, thousands more soldiers would die or the Allies might lose the war. So scientists proposed exploding the test bomb inside a giant steel vessel. If the bomb did not explode, the plutonium could be retrieved and used again. A company in Ohio agreed to build the steel container. It would be twenty-five feet long, twelve feet in diameter, and fourteen inches thick. "Jumbo," as it became known, would weigh 214 tons.

In the meantime, Groves looked for a place to test Fat Man in secret. His advisors suggested eight possible locations, ranging from sandbars off the coast of Texas to an island in Southern California. A few places closer to Los Alamos were also considered, including the San Luis Valley of Colorado and an area near Grants, New Mexico.

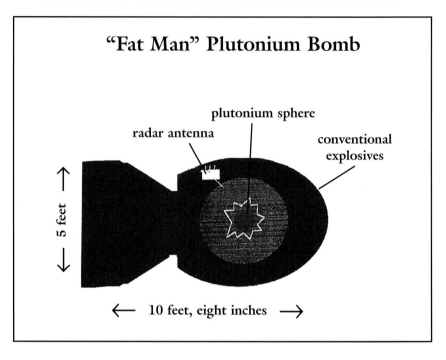

"Fat Man" Plutonium Bomb

plutonium sphere

radar antenna

conventional explosives

5 feet

← 10 feet, eight inches →

"Fat Man" was a complicated bomb that contained several conventional explosives that were all set to go off at the same moment. When they did, they compressed plutonium inside a sphere until it exploded.

The Allies Reclaim France

While Groves considered the advantages of each site, the leaders of the Allied military forces searched for a different kind of site. They were looking for a place to land troops and tanks on mainland Europe so they could begin an assault on Germany. Military leaders studied various spots along the coast of France.

The history books call June 6, 1944, "D-Day." This was the day the Allies stormed Europe from the shore at Normandy, France. German leaders had prepared for just such an attack, and its army was waiting—but at the wrong place! German forces were at Calais, a place north and east of Normandy. Consequently, the Allies were able to land on the beaches of France and began pushing the German Army out of the European countries it had invaded.

The United States was also making progress in the fight against Japan. In one battle near the island of Guam, more than three quarters of the Japanese air force was destroyed. Yet the Japanese fought on.

By now, Groves had chosen a site near Alamagordo, New Mexico, for Fat Man's test. This desert area already held the Alamagordo Bombing Range, a United States military base where explosives were tested. The site had other advantages as well. The nearest inhabitant lived twelve miles away, and Carrizozo, the closest town, was twenty-seven miles away. In addition, Alamagordo was only two hundred miles from Los Alamos. The Manhattan Project would use an eighteen-by-twenty-four-mile section at the northwest corner of the base. Oppenheimer dubbed this site "Trinity" after a passage in a poem called "Hymne to God My God, in My Sicknesse," by John Donne.

Allied forces liberated Paris on August 25, then pushed on toward Germany. Close behind them came a special team of men called "Alsos." The Alsos examined deserted German labs to determine how close to completion the German atomic bomb was. By fall, the team had decided that Germany did not possess a nuclear weapon.

In November 1944, President Roosevelt became the first United States president to be elected to a fourth term in office. The next month, bulldozers and construction crews arrived at Trinity to construct a base camp. Soldiers came to guard it. Most found the land harsh and lonely. Rattlesnakes and tarantulas skittered across the sand. Once, a B-29 (a military plane used for bombing) swooped over the site. It had come from the main base, and the soldiers inside decided to use the antelope below for target practice. They were completely unaware that people were down there, too. Trinity soldiers ran for cover. Luckily, no one was hurt.[6]

Soldiers in the Pacific were involved in much fiercer battles. The fight for the Philippine Islands lasted all fall and winter, but the islands were finally liberated from the Japanese in early March 1945. Other soldiers were fighting on the island of Iwo Jima. This would be the bloodiest battle of the war against Japan. Iwo Jima is only five miles long and less than two miles wide. Even so, more than six thousand men died while capturing it. The Allies finally won the island on March 16. Now United States troops headed for the island of Okinawa. The Allies were finally making progress pushing Japanese forces back toward Japan. But the war was far from over.

FINAL PREPARATIONS

By April 1945, the Allies had advanced into German territory. Soon they discovered that Hitler's concentration camps had become huge death camps for men, women, and children from the countries the Nazis had invaded. Most of the prisoners at these camps were Jewish. But Hitler had also ordered thousands of gypsies, Poles, and Slavs to be imprisoned. These captives had been forced to live and work in horrible conditions. Many had died from starvation, overwork, and cruel treatment. Thousands more had been tortured to death.

Hitler's Genocide Is Discovered

These camps held an even darker secret. Several of them had gas chambers that had been built to look like shower facilities. Camp guards regularly ordered groups of prisoners into the chambers to "take a shower." But the doors were then locked, and poisonous gas was piped into the room. The victims inside had no way of escaping and eventually died from the poisonous fumes. The bodies were then burned. This process was repeated over and over again at the camps in an effort to carry out Hitler's plan to rid the world of Jews and other "undesirables."

Most of the world knew nothing about these murder camps until the Allies reached them in the spring of 1945. The thousands of prisoners they found alive were given immediate medical attention. By then, 11 million people had already been murdered by the Nazis. Six million of them had been Jewish. This was more than two thirds of Europe's total Jewish population. Hitler's attempt to exterminate the Jewish population during World War II is known as the Holocaust.

The 509th

As headlines reported one concentration camp horror after another, a group of American pilots was being trained at Wendover Field in Utah. These pilots made up the 509th Composite Group. They had been sent to Wendover to prepare for the dropping of the world's first atomic bomb.

Of course, the men of the 509th knew nothing about the Manhattan Project. They knew only that they were training for a secret mission involving special B-29 bombers. Every day, they flew over a designated route, dropped a fake bomb at a target, and then flew away as fast as they could. The scientists at Los Alamos had calculated that the airplane that dropped the real bomb would have to travel eight miles in forty-three seconds to escape being destroyed by the explosion. The commander of the 509th, Colonel Paul W. Tibbets, Jr., made it clear that he expected perfection on each training flight. Any pilot who returned just five minutes late was in trouble.[1]

Meanwhile, construction crews were finishing a new air base on the Pacific island of Tinian. Tinian was similar in size and shape to New York City's Manhattan Island. Consequently, soldiers were soon naming Tinian's streets after famous Manhattan landmarks. There was a Fifth Avenue, a 125th Street, and even a Times Square.

Trinity Goes Into Operation

Back in the United States, Kenneth Bainbridge became the director of the Trinity site. Scientists and technicians were now arriving there daily, getting the base ready for the big test. Truckloads of equipment were also arriving daily. Yet the base did not always receive the supplies it needed the most. This forced the soldiers at Trinity to improvise. For instance, when poles needed for stringing electrical cables across the desert did not come, the men strung the cables from tall cactus plants.

The scientists had another concern: radioactive fallout. Fallout is material that is released into the air or deposited on the earth's surface after a nuclear explosion. Exposure to a large amount of radioactive fallout can cause immediate sickness or death. Even a little can cause serious health problems if someone is exposed to it for a long enough time. Fallout can also contaminate soil and water, and then be transferred to plants, animals, and people. After studying the issue, scientists concluded that the bomb would not "poison an area of more than a few square kilometers."[2] But this was really just a guess. No one knew for sure how much fallout would be released by the bomb. Therefore, scientists advised Bainbridge to make plans for evacuating people from the area in case the test released a lot of radiation.

Truman Becomes President

On April 12, 1945, President Roosevelt died suddenly of a cerebral hemorrhage. Hours later, Vice President Harry Truman was sworn in as the new president. He later said that, at the moment, he felt as if "the moon, the stars, and all the planets had fallen" on him.[3] Yet he still had no knowledge of the Manhattan Project. Groves had kept the mission so secret that even the vice president had not been informed of its existence. Neither had General Dwight D. Eisenhower, the commander of the military forces in Europe, or General Douglas MacArthur, the man in charge of the Pacific troops.

It was Secretary of War Henry Stimson who told President Truman about the Manhattan Project. Stimson reported that, within four months, the United States would have developed "the most terrible weapon ever known in human history, one bomb of which could destroy a whole city."[4] Stimson went on to tell Truman that atomic power could conceivably destroy modern civilization.

Hitler Is Defeated

By now, the Alsos had issued another report about Germany's atomic bomb project. The report stated that German research in 1940 and 1941 had kept pace with American research. But in the summer of 1942, German physicists accidentally destroyed their first nuclear reactor. After that, the Germans were never close to the United States in building a working bomb.

With the Allies closing in on Berlin, Germany, the war in Europe was finally coming to an end. Realizing that he was defeated, Adolf Hitler committed suicide on April 30, 1945. German leaders officially surrendered on May 7, 1945. But World War II was not over. The United States was still battling Japan, with no end in sight.

The War in the Pacific

By May 1945, B-29s were taking off at regular intervals from the new air base at Tinian, now the largest airfield in the world. One soldier later described the base as an amazingly efficient war machine:

> At sunset some days the field would be loud with the roar of motors. Down the great runways would roll the huge planes, seeming to move slowly because of their size, but far outspeeding the occasional racing jeep. One after another, each runway would launch its planes. Once every fifteen seconds another B-29 would become air-borne. For an hour and a half this would continue with precision and order.[5]

All these planes were headed to Japan to drop conventional bombs. In one attack alone, 124,000 people in Tokyo were killed. Japanese factories were being destroyed, and Japanese ships were being sunk. The country was near ruin. But its leaders still refused to surrender. In fact, some Japanese soldiers were so dedicated to their cause that they deliberately crashed their airplanes into United States battleships. These men were called kamikaze pilots, and they knew their actions would severely damage United States ships. They also knew the crash would kill them. But each one considered his cause more important than his life.

Actions such as these made United States military strategists wonder if their bombing raids would ever defeat Japan. Plans were made for a land invasion of Japan to take place in November 1945. Leaders predicted this attack would cost thousands more lives. A second attack was planned for March 1946, if needed.

These leaders still did not know about the mission meant for the 509th Composite Group. Neither did the regular soldiers at Tinian. But everyone had noticed the special group of pilots. Many people suspected that they were involved in a top-secret operation. Soon, the 509th became known as the Glory Boys. Someone wrote a poem in their honor:

> *Into the air the secret rose.*
> *Where they're going, nobody knows.*
> *Tomorrow they'll return again.*
> *But we'll never know where they've been.*
> *Don't ask us about results or such,*
> *Unless you want to get in Dutch.*
> *But take it from one who is sure of the score.*
> *The 509th is winning the war.*[6]

Preparing for Fat Man's Test

On May 7, 1945, one hundred tons of TNT were exploded at Trinity as a drill for the upcoming test of Fat Man. The practice gave scientists a chance to try out their instruments and check their procedures. Now work proceeded at a feverish pace, and everyone worked eighteen hours a day. Anyone with a spare moment made face masks in preparation for the blast. These were nothing more than aluminum sheets fitted with welder's goggles and mounted on a stick.

This makeshift army camp in the New Mexico desert housed the scientists and soldiers who would help test the first atomic bomb.

The Fat Man atomic bomb would be exploded from a one-hundred-foot steel tower that had been built ten miles from base camp. This was called Ground Zero. Roads linked Ground Zero to various observation bunkers in the surrounding desert. Hundreds of miles of wire connected radios and switches from each of the dugouts to the tower and to each other. The closest three bunkers were more than five miles from the tower, and the one to the south would be the control station.

Jumbo sat nearby, having completed its journey from Ohio. It had come by train, truck, and three caterpillar tractors. But by the time it arrived, scientists had decided not to use it. Plutonium production was steady and everyone felt confident that the bomb would work.

Now Manhattan Project leaders looked for the best date to test the bomb. They wanted a clear, calm day to ensure quality photographs and lessen the spread of fallout. Furthermore, rain could destroy the bomb's firing mechanism. After consulting meteorologists, they chose July 16. The bomb would be detonated at 4:00 A.M. so that few uninvolved citizens would see it.

An Important Decision

As the war continued, some of the scientists who had helped make the bomb now wondered if it should even be used. Many had helped invent the bomb in order to defeat Hitler. Since Germany had lost the war, some believed that there was no reason to unleash such a

This sphere of plutonium was all that was needed to create Fat Man.

terrible weapon. Leo Szilard, the man who had helped convince President Roosevelt to begin the Manhattan Project, was one of them. He wrote to President Truman and urged him not to use the bomb. Sixty-seven other scientists signed his letter. The letter, however, was intercepted by security officials and never delivered.[7]

Yet these scientists' opinions were considered. A group of people called the Interim Committee had been formed to discuss whether or not the bomb should be used against Japan. Some of the committee members wanted to demonstrate the bomb. They hoped that this would save lives while encouraging the Japanese to surrender. But other members pointed to flaws in this plan. For example, if the demonstration were not conducted in Japan, its leaders might think the bomb was some kind of a trick. If it were demonstrated in Japan, there was the chance that the Japanese military would shoot down the plane carrying the bomb, or that the Japanese would take American war prisoners to the demonstration site. A few committee members wondered what would happen if the bomb failed.

Fat Man had several wires leading from the conventional explosives inside the bomb.

The Interim Committee finally recommended that the bomb be used as if it were any other weapon of war. Of course, this was only advice. President Truman would make the final decision about whether or not to use the bomb.

On July 9, a model of Fat Man was driven over rocky roads for eight hours to see if the real bomb could withstand the rough trip from Los Alamos to Trinity. It performed perfectly. That same day, Oppenheimer wrote an invitation to fellow scientists Ernest Lawrence and Arthur Compton: "Any time after the 15th would be good for our fishing trip. Because we are not certain of the weather, we may be delayed several days. We do not have enough sleeping bags to go around, so we ask you please not to bring anyone with you."[8] Lawrence and Compton understood that Oppenheimer was not really talking about fishing. He was notifying his friends of the bomb's test date and inviting them to come and watch.

8

TEST DAY FOR FAT MAN

On July 12, 1945, Fat Man started its journey to Trinity. It would travel in two major parts. The first part was the nuclear core, still unassembled. It was packed into the backseat of an army car, with Philip Morrison, a physicist, next to it. This car would travel between one filled with security men and another loaded with scientists. They left Los Alamos at about 3:00 P.M. and arrived at Trinity at 8:00 P.M. The core was taken directly to an abandoned ranch house on the site.

Back in Los Alamos, the part of the bomb that contained the conventional explosives was being checked by X ray. Everything was in order, so it was placed in a wooden crate and carefully lifted onto a truck. The transport crew drew straws to see who would sit with the crate to steady it during the ride.[1] Soon the truck was on its way with a five-vehicle escort.

At 9:00 A.M. on July 13, eight men entered the ranch house on the Trinity site to put together the nuclear core. Geiger counters, instruments used to

Scientists gently lift Fat Man's plutonium core from the car that brought it from Los Alamos to Trinity.

measure radiation, were set up to monitor the makeshift lab. Military police waited outside. Their four jeeps faced outward, engines running, ready for an emergency getaway.

The other part of the bomb had arrived at the tower, and by 3:30 P.M., it was ready for the core. Scientists brought the core from the ranch house and began lowering it inch by inch into the bomb casing. Sweat dripped from their faces. Everyone knew that the tiniest wrong move could start an unstoppable chain reaction. When the winds picked up and lightning streaked the sky, the men grew even more nervous—either lightning or wind could set off a deadly explosion.[2] But the work continued. Once the core was inside the casing, the final explosives were put into place. One ill-fitting charge was secured with ordinary cellophane tape.[3] The bomb was completely assembled by 10:00 P.M.

Fat Man Goes up the Tower

At 8:00 the next morning, scientists began hoisting the bomb up the tower. Realizing what would happen if the cable holding it broke, they immediately ordered a new mission. "Operation Mattress" sent soldiers hurrying about the base, collecting mattresses, which were then stacked twelve feet high beneath the bomb. Hopefully, if the bomb fell, the mattresses would soften the impact enough to prevent an explosion.[4]

As the bomb was being raised to the top of the tower, Alvin and Elizabeth Graves were checking into a motel in Carrizozo, the closest town to the test site. The Graveses were posing as travelers, but they were really scientists assigned to monitor the radioactive fallout from the test. Once inside their room, they set up a Geiger counter, seismograph, shortwave radio, and portable generator for electricity. If the fallout level in Carrizozo rose too high, the Graveses would report it. Then nearby soldiers would knock on every door in town and load every citizen into an army truck to be rushed to safety. Despite all their calculations, none of the scientists really knew what might happen. Some even wondered if the whole world might end.

Scientists carefully hoist Fat Man up the tower at Trinity.

In fact, many were now placing bets on how successful Fat Man would be. Oppenheimer put his money on a yield as powerful as three hundred tons of TNT. Bethe chose eight thousand tons. Half-jokingly, Fermi was asking scientists if they thought the explosion would destroy the whole world or just all of New Mexico. As for Groves, he worried about what he would tell his superiors if the countdown reached zero and nothing happened.[5]

Little Boy Begins Its Journey

Meanwhile, Little Boy was leaving Los Alamos on its long journey to Tinian. This was the uranium bomb that scientists felt sure would explode. Seven carloads of guards, two army officers, and a doctor drove it to Kirtland Air Base in Albuquerque. There, it was loaded onto an airplane bound for San Francisco. Groves ordered a second airplane to follow the first. The bomb's special uranium was still scarce, and enough uranium for another one would not be available for months. If the first plane crashed, Groves reasoned, the second plane could report its location and the U-235 could be recovered.

Both planes landed safely in San Francisco, and the top-secret cargo was transferred to *Indianapolis*, the ship that would transport the bomb to Tinian. The men in charge of the bomb had strict orders that, if anything happened to the ship, they were to save the uranium at all costs. As one writer put it, "If the *Indianapolis* sank, the first life raft would go to the U-235."[6]

Rained Out?

At Trinity, the moment of truth for Fat Man was less than forty-eight hours away. Three years of preparation, secrecy, and eighteen-hour workdays were coming to an end. Soon scientists would have an answer to the biggest question of the century: Was a nuclear weapon possible? July 15 was tense with waiting. Some people tried to relax with an outing to local abandoned mines. Others finished preparations or conducted practices on their equipment. The photography crew set up cameras. Near dusk all the activities wound down. The test was only hours away.

Then it started to rain. Both Groves and Oppenheimer knew the test would have to be postponed. Rain, wind, or lightning could disrupt the mechanical workings of the bomb or increase the level of fallout. Some scientists wanted to wait a full twenty-four hours. But each delay complicated the project. First of all, the men at the base were nearing exhaustion. Every passing moment compromised their clear thinking. Second, Groves knew that President Truman was awaiting news about the test in order to formulate important political strategies. Each moment he did not know if the weapon worked prolonged the war and cost lives. Finally, any postponement increased the chance of sabotage or discovery. Groves and Oppenheimer knew they must wait until the weather cleared, but they decided to proceed at the first minute possible. Outside, the thunder boomed, lightning cracked, and rain poured from the skies.

When the storm finally let up around 4:00 A.M., Groves set the new detonation time for 5:30 A.M. Scientists and soldiers quickly moved into their assigned positions. Ground Zero was evacuated except for a small group of men who climbed up the tower to make the final connections. Then they turned on huge floodlights to help guide airplanes that would photograph the event. At 5:00 A.M., they climbed down the tower and headed for cover.

At the control center, Bainbridge opened a padlocked box that held the bomb's firing switch. He had the only key that had been made for the lock. Bainbridge moved the switch to the ready position, and the bomb was armed.

At 5:10 A.M., Trinity's public address system blared out "The Star-Spangled Banner," and an announcement was made: "It is now zero minus twenty minutes."

Men crowded into the control center to monitor various dials and switches. One synchronized his watch by telephone with an army major in Santa Fe, who would be in charge of the operation if Trinity were blown up. A chemist named Donald Hornig sat with his hand on the switch that would stop the test if necessary. Oppenheimer stood behind him, nervously watching it all.[7]

Tension increased as the countdown was broadcast in minutes. Then it came in seconds. At forty-five seconds to detonation, physicist Joseph McKibben threw a switch to start the automatic timer inside the bomb.

At zero minus thirty seconds, men all over the base braced themselves for the impending explosion. Groves lay on the ground outside base camp, the closest point from which anyone was allowed to view the bomb outdoors.

Success!

At 5:29 A.M., the world's first nuclear bomb exploded. Instantly, the gray morning became a blinding white light. Groves described the bomb as being as bright as "several suns in midday."[8] Another army general reported that it "was golden, purple, violet, gray and blue," lighting every peak and ridge of the surrounding mountains with beauty.[9]

A roar that sounded like a freight train rumbled through the area for the next five minutes. It was so loud that it woke up people in Carrizozo. Some looked out of their windows to see a tower of fire rising six miles into the air. The Graveses felt their motel room shake. The major in Santa Fe saw a flash of light in the sky. In Roswell, New Mexico, residents wondered if a meteor had struck the earth.[10] Windows were even blown out in Gallup, New Mexico, 235 miles northwest of Trinity.[11]

At Trinity, observers watched as the fireball grew into a churning mushroom-shaped cloud of smoke. In ten minutes, the cloud was breaking into three separate pieces, and in half an hour each was dissipating. The Manhattan Project had been a success! The scientists were elated and congratulated one another with hugs

SOURCE DOCUMENT

... WHEN THE SHOT WENT OFF, EVEN THOUGH WE HAD VERY, VERY DARK GLASSES IN FRONT OF OUR EYES, THE MOUNTAINS LIT UP TO THE SOUTH JUST AS IF IT WERE DAYLIGHT. WE FELT THE HEAT ON THE BACK OF OUR NECKS. WHEN WE TURNED AROUND THERE WAS THIS HUGE BALL OF FIRE GOING UP INTO THE AIR. IT SEEMED LIKE IT WAS GOING UP AND UP AND UP AND THEN THE LIGHT DROPPED IN INTENSITY BUT THE CLOUD CONTINUED TO GO WAY UP. THERE WAS ENOUGH DAYLIGHT BY THEN THAT WE COULD WATCH THE CLOUD GO ALL THE WAY UP IN THE AIR. A VERY STRANGE THING HAPPENED. THERE'S A THING CALLED A "DUST DEVIL" IN THIS COUNTRY, WHICH IS A VERY SMALL TORNADO. . . . AFTER THE CLOUD DISAPPEARED, A DUST DEVIL APPEARED IN THE TRINITY CRATER. IT DIDN'T MOVE ACROSS THE COUNTRYSIDE LIKE THEY USUALLY DO, IT JUST STAYED THERE, AND IT STAYED THERE ABOUT AN HOUR. . . .[12]

Physicist Robert Krohn was present for the Trinity test and gave this account of what he saw there.

and howls.[13] One soldier summed up the explosion by telling a fellow observer, "You just saw the end of the war."[14]

Parties were soon sent out to analyze the explosion. They found no tower. The bomb had evaporated it. In its place was a twelve-hundred-foot-wide crater filled with green pebbles of glass. The bomb's heat had sucked up the desert soil and fused it into these emerald-colored beads, beads that would become known as trinitite. Jumbo had been tipped over. The only sign of animal life was the carbonized shadows that had been etched onto stones or the soil. Yucca plants, Joshua trees, cactus plants—all were gone. Scientists later calculated the bomb's power to have been equal to fifteen thousand tons of TNT.

William Lawrence, a science reporter for *The New York Times*, had been hired by Groves to write about the event for the army. He was the only newspaper reporter allowed at Trinity. He would echo what many were thinking when he wrote that the test was

> fascinating and terrifying . . . full of great promise and great foreboding. . . . It was as though the earth had opened and the skies split. One felt as though he had been privileged to witness the birth of the world—to be present at the moment of creation when the Lord said: "Let there be light."[15]

But Oppenheimer was thinking more about destruction than creation. A different quote crossed his mind, words from an ancient poem: "I am Death—the shatterer of worlds."[16] Then he walked into the desert to be alone and came upon a turtle that had been flipped on its back by the shock wave. He bent down and set it upright.

9

UNLEASHING THE ULTIMATE WEAPON

As scientists were watching the explosion at Trinity, President Harry Truman was meeting with British Prime Minister Winston Churchill and Soviet Premier Joseph Stalin in Potsdam, Germany. The Allied leaders had gathered to discuss terms for a peace treaty with Germany. On July 17, 1945, Truman received a coded message from Secretary of War Henry Stimson. "Operated on this morning. Diagnosis not yet complete but results seem satisfactory and already exceed expectations."[1] Truman understood that the Trinity test had gone well, and he was delighted.

Truman's Decision

Churchill, who was well aware of the Manhattan Project, had also been awaiting news of Trinity's success. He was as happy to hear the news as Truman was. "Now all this nightmare picture had vanished," Churchill said. "In its place was the vision of the end of the whole war in one or two violent shocks."[2]

Truman and Churchill discussed how and when to tell Stalin that the United States had developed an atomic bomb. Both leaders worried that, despite their wartime alliance, the Soviets would not always be friendly. This made the United States and Great Britain reluctant to share any top-secret information with Stalin.

As Truman considered this issue, a larger decision loomed on the horizon: Should the new weapon be used? Some people argued that the atomic bomb would save more people than it killed by ending the war quickly. Truman later reported that he was told a Japanese invasion would cost between 250,000 and 500,000 United States casualties. Indeed, he was not the only one who seemed anxious to end the war. Billboards such as the one outside Oak Ridge, Tennessee, were seen all across the United States. It read: "Whose Son Will Die in the Last Minute of the War? Minutes Count!"

But other advisors were not as eager to use the new weapon. Admiral William D. Leahy, for example, thought it was "a barbarous weapon."[3] Secretary of War Stimson was also bothered by the bomb. He called it diabolical. He urged Truman to use it only against military targets so that innocent civilians would not be hurt.[4]

As for Groves, it was his job to be ready for a nuclear strike if he was ordered to make one. So he continued preparations. Three B-29s would deliver the bomb: One would carry the weapon and the other two would photograph the event. Now three B-29s regularly flew over Japan without making any kind of an attack. Military strategists hoped that Japanese anti-aircraft gunners would come to identify three lone B-29s as harmless. This might prevent the trio that actually brought the bomb from being shot down.

On July 24, Truman finally told Stalin about the successful new weapon. This might prevent Stalin from complaining later that the United States and Great Britain had been keeping secrets from him. But Truman mentioned few details, only assuring the Soviet leader that the bomb was extremely destructive. Stalin quietly replied that he hoped the United States would make "good use of it against the Japanese."[5] His unenthusiastic response left Truman wondering if Stalin knew that he was referring to an atomic weapon. Most historians believe that Stalin had indeed under-stood the implications of Truman's comment. Some even think that Stalin's spies had informed him of Trinity's success before Truman himself had received the news.[6]

The next day, July 25, 1945, President Truman signed an order for the 509th Composite Group to drop an atomic bomb on Japan as soon as possible after August 3, 1945, allowing time for the order to be changed. Then Truman gave the Japanese one last opportunity to surrender. On July 26, the United States and Great Britain issued an ultimatum that became known as the Potsdam Declaration. The declaration demanded that Japan surrender unconditionally or face destruction.

Japan Responds

As leaders waited for the Japanese response, the *Indianapolis* unloaded its top-secret cargo at Tinian. Scientists from Los Alamos were already waiting at the base to start assembling Little Boy. They began their work as the ship headed back out to sea.

Japanese leaders responded to the Potsdam Declaration on July 28. They refused to surrender. As if to underscore their decision, a Japanese submarine torpedoed the *Indianapolis* the next day near the island of Leyte. The *Indianapolis* sank, and 880 American soldiers lost their lives.

Four days later, Truman was aboard the *Augusta* on his way back to Washington, D.C. On the way, he sent out the order for an atomic bomb to be dropped. Four cities—Hiroshima, Kokura, Nagasaki, and Niigata—had been identified as possible targets and ranked in order of preference. Hiroshima was first on the list.

Bombing Hiroshima

Hiroshima was vital to the Japanese war effort. It housed over forty-three thousand soldiers and was filled with factories that produced military hardware. Furthermore, Hiroshima was the place from which the Japanese launched attacks on its Asian neighbors. But Hiroshima was also the home of approximately two hundred eighty thousand civilians.

On August 6, the Glory Boys of the 509th were finally called into action. At 2:45 that morning, Commander Tibbets taxied the *Enola Gay*, a B-29 he had named after his mother, down a Tinian runway. Inside were twelve other men of the 509th Composite, and a partially assembled uranium bomb. The bomb would be finished in-flight, a precaution meant to save the Tinian airbase from destruction if something went wrong during takeoff. When the plane was safely in the air, Tibbets informed his crew that they were carrying an atomic weapon. Captain William S. Parsons had already begun putting it together.

At 7:30 A.M., Parsons reported that the bomb was ready. By 9:10 A.M., Hiroshima was in sight and Tibbets had found his target, the Aioi Bridge. As hoped, no one on the ground had been alarmed by the three B-29s. Therefore, no alarms were sounded, no one sought shelter, and no attacks on the B-29s were ordered.

At 9:15 A.M., six miles above the city, the *Enola Gay* released the first atomic bomb ever used in war. Forty-five seconds later, one piece of uranium collided with another, and the most powerful weapon known to humankind exploded nineteen hundred feet above the earth. By then, the *Enola Gay* was seven miles away and nearly twenty-eight thousand feet above it. Even so, two strong shock waves from the explosion rocked the plane. Tibbets maneuvered through the turbulence, then circled back to look at Hiroshima.

Colonel Paul Tibbets piloted the Enola Gay, *the plane that dropped the atomic bomb on Hiroshima.*

The bomb had exploded over a hospital courtyard, missing its target by five hundred fifty feet. It mattered little. The city below had disappeared. In its place was a mass of bubbling purple-gray smoke. Copilot Robert Lewis later reported that he had actually tasted the fissioning atoms, and that they had tasted like lead. After observing the explosion, he wrote in his diary, "My God, what have we done?"[7]

Death and Destruction

Every living thing within a half-mile radius of ground zero had been killed instantly, including at least seventy thousand people. Those who survived the initial blast saw a flash of blinding light, felt a rush of searing air, and heard a deafening roar. Thousands of people were struck by flying debris. Thousands more were burned by heat ranging from 5,400 to 7,200 degrees. This heat was so intense that it melted the skin from some people's bodies. Most of them soon died.

Within minutes, the intense heat ignited fires all across the city. Wind from the blast soon whipped the individual fires into one huge blaze. This firestorm killed thousands more people. Then came the "black rain," radioactive fallout blackened by carbon ash. The black rain killed some people immediately; others would not die for months. By the end of the day, charred bodies lay everywhere. By the end of the year, the death count caused by the bomb had risen to one hundred forty thousand.

Smoke from the first atomic bomb used in war billows 20,000 feet over Hiroshima, Japan, in August 1945.

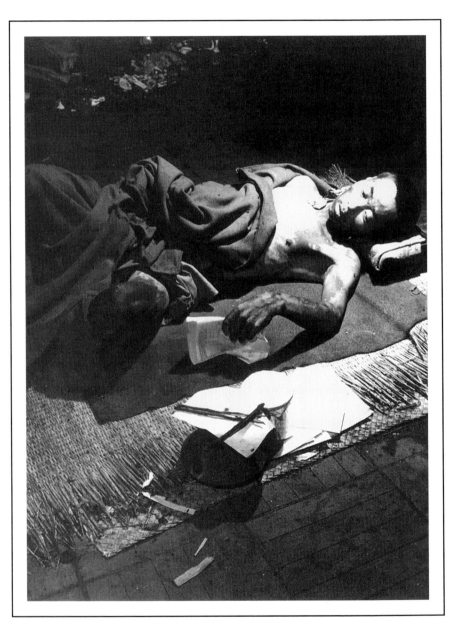

Survivors of the atomic blast suffered burns, blindness, and radiation poisoning.

In a matter of minutes, the bomb had vaporized, flattened, and twisted seventy thousand buildings. Hiroshima's houses, shops, hospitals, fire departments, and police stations had disappeared. Roads, vehicles, and water systems had been destroyed. This made any kind of organized rescue effort impossible.

The World Learns About the Bomb

In Washington, D.C., Groves decoded the top-secret message he had been waiting to hear—the *Enola Gay*'s mission had been a success. He immediately relayed the news to his superiors. A message went out to President Truman, who was still aboard the *Augusta*. Truman jubilantly told some sailors, "This is the greatest thing in history."[8] The president soon released a public statement about the attack, telling the world about the new weapon that had been used against the Japanese. The bomb, he said, had been as powerful as twenty thousand tons of TNT, a force two thousand times greater than any bomb ever used before. Truman then promised a "rain of ruin" upon Japan if it did not surrender.

Ironically, the Japanese officials who heard Truman's report dismissed it as propaganda. Because the bomb had wiped out all communication systems in Hiroshima, they had no idea what had happened. It would be twenty-four hours before they received the news: Half of Hiroshima no longer existed.

★10★

THE WAR FOR PEACE

As Japanese leaders learned of Hiroshima's destruction, thousands of United States citizens were finally learning what they had been building. People in Oak Ridge handed over dollar bills for three-cent newspapers, just to read the details of how their factory had helped make a new bomb. The Santa Fe newspaper was laying to rest rumors that people on the mesa had been working on gas warfare or making windshield wipers for submarines. Even Leslie Groves's wife was finding out for the first time what project had been keeping her husband away from home.

All over the United States, people read President Truman's praise for the scientists who had created the bomb. He called the atomic bomb "the greatest achievement of organized science in history."[1]

Japan Continues to Fight

But in Tokyo, Japanese leaders decided to keep fighting. Hoping to encourage a change of heart, United States airplanes dropped millions of leaflets over Japanese cities that described the United States' new weapon. The flyers, written in Japanese, said that the new bomb was "the most destructive explosive ever devised by man . . . we ask that you now petition the Emperor to end the war. . . . Otherwise, we shall resolutely employ this bomb and all our other superior weapons to promptly and forcefully end the war."[2]

On August 8, 1945, the Soviet Union declared war on Japan and began to drive the Japanese Army out of Manchuria. Still, the Japanese did not surrender.

The Bomb at Nagasaki

On August 9, Captain Frederick C. Bock of the 509th Composite took off from Tinian. His B-29 was carrying a plutonium bomb identical to the one that had been tested at Trinity. Clouds covered the targeted city of Kokura, so Bock proceeded to his next target, Nagasaki. At 10:58 A.M., Bock piloted his plane through a break in the clouds and released the bomb over Nagasaki.

This atomic bomb exploded with a force equal to twenty-one thousand tons of TNT. Nearly forty thousand people died within seconds of its detonation. Then came the "black rain" that had fallen on Hiroshima. As in Hiroshima, rescue efforts were useless due to destroyed buildings, roads, and communication systems.

Japan Surrenders

The bombing of Nagasaki finally convinced Japanese leaders that the United States might really be able to destroy their nation. Japan surrendered to the Allies on August 10, 1945, unaware that there was only one more nuclear bomb ready for use. On August 14, the word was official: World War II was over. It had been the bloodiest war ever fought. Seventeen million soldiers had been killed in the fighting, and at least twice as many civilians had died. Eleven million had been victims of Hitler's genocide. Millions more had been

SOURCE DOCUMENT

WE HEREBY PROCLAIM THE UNCONDITIONAL SURRENDER TO THE ALLIED POWERS OF THE JAPANESE IMPERIAL GENERAL HEADQUARTERS AND OF ALL JAPANESE ARMED FORCES AND ALL ARMED FORCES UNDER JAPANESE CONTROL WHEREVER SITUATED.

WE HEREBY COMMAND ALL JAPANESE ARMED FORCES WHEREVER SITUATED AND THE JAPANESE PEOPLE TO CEASE HOSTILITIES FORTHWITH, TO PRESERVE AND SAVE FROM DAMAGE ALL SHIPS, AIRCRAFT, AND MILITARY AND CIVIL PROPERTY AND TO COMPLY WITH ALL REQUIREMENTS WHICH MAY BE IMPOSED BY THE SUPREME COMMANDER FOR THE ALLIED POWERS OR BY AGENCIES OF THE JAPANESE GOVERNMENT AT HIS DIRECTION. . . .

THE AUTHORITY OF THE EMPEROR AND THE JAPANESE GOVERNMENT TO RULE THE STATE SHALL BE SUBJECT TO THE SUPREME COMMANDER FOR THE ALLIED POWERS WHO WILL TAKE SUCH STEPS AS HE DEEMS PROPER TO EFFECTUATE THESE TERMS OF SURRENDER.[3]

Only after the devastation of Hiroshima and Nagasaki by American atomic bombs did the Japanese decide to surrender to the Allied forces.

killed by wartime bombing. Thousands of others had died from famine or disease brought on by the war.

The news of the war's end sent the entire United States population into jubilant celebration. For many, surrender meant that their loved ones were coming home. In New York City, half a million elated citizens jammed Times Square. A conga line wound its way across the lawn in front of the White House. People danced at Los Alamos, too, as scientists set off leftover explosives in the canyon below. Soldiers everywhere cried with relief. They knew that their odds of growing old had just improved dramatically.

United States forces landed in Japan on August 28. By the end of the next day, Allied warships were anchored in Tokyo Bay with their weapons pointed at the Japanese shore. On September 2, eleven Japanese leaders stepped onto the deck of the *Missouri* to surrender formally. American General Douglas MacArthur officiated at the proceedings. It took twenty minutes for the representatives of all involved nations to sign the documents. MacArthur ended the proceedings by saying, "Let us pray that peace be now restored to the world and that God will preserve it always."[4]

Surveying the Atomic Destruction

During the first two weeks of September, a team of investigators from the United States arrived in Japan. This group was called the Manhattan Atomic Bomb Investigating Group. It had two missions. First, the team was to determine whether the Japanese had been working on a nuclear weapon. The team reported that, although the Japanese had been studying fission, its scientists were not close to developing an atomic bomb.

The team's second mission was to examine Hiroshima and Nagasaki. It first measured radiation levels in these cities, and determined that there was no unusual level of radiation from the ground. But the destruction and injury they found at the sites were horrifying.

At ground zero, the bomb's brightness had etched the shapes of people and animals into hard stone an instant before incinerating them. One young officer named Osborn Elliot described the scene:

> As you stand in the middle of town, for miles on every side nothing rises above the level of your knees except for the shell of a building or the grotesque skeleton of a tree or perhaps a mound where the rubble has been pushed into a pile. . . . How anybody was left alive, I do not know. But here and there, women and children were sitting on the rubble that was once their homes. . . . Many people had sores on their faces. We stared at them, and they gazed blankly back at us.[5]

Elliot commented that the men in his unit felt no remorse, only pity: "In our view, the atom bomb had saved many thousands of lives—quite possibly including our own."[6]

Guilt Settles Over the Scientists

Before long, the news of the horrors caused by the atomic bombs dampened the elation of victory. Congratulations for the scientists were soon being replaced with criticisms. Some people felt that Japan had been close to surrender and that the bombs had been unnecessary. *Time* magazine quoted several people who felt the bomb was inhumane. One man called it "mass murder, sheer terrorism."[7] Even Enrico Fermi received a letter from his sister that criticized him for participating in the bomb effort.[8] Although the majority of Americans supported the bombings, these negative words brought gloom on the Los Alamos scientists. It worsened when scientist Harry Daghlian died. Daghlian had been accidentally exposed to a large amount of radiation in August. (Physicist Louis Slotin would die in the spring from the same cause.)

Soon, many Manhattan Project scientists were feeling guilty for having helped make a nuclear weapon.[9] Hundreds returned to the universities or laboratories where they had worked before the war. Others took new positions. At its peak, Los Alamos had supported three thousand people. By October 1945, only a thousand remained. Oppenheimer resigned, too, predicting that "If atomic bombs are to be added to the arsenals of a warring world . . . then the time will come when mankind will curse the names of Los Alamos and Hiroshima."[10]

In the meantime, General MacArthur commanded an occupation force of United States soldiers in Japan. These soldiers helped clean up the destroyed Japanese cities. They provided medical aid and food to the needy. MacArthur was also in charge of dismantling the Japanese military and helping the Japanese form a democratic government.

A New Nuclear Weapon

The Manhattan Engineering District officially ended on January 1, 1947. It had spent over $1.8 billion— about $20 billion in today's money.[11] But the nuclear laboratories at Los Alamos were never closed. The government believed that an atomic research center was vital to United States security, and Los Alamos was the perfect place for one. Norris E. Bradbury became its director, and his work was overseen by a newly formed agency called the Atomic Energy Commission (AEC). The AEC had been formed by Congress in 1946. Soon the AEC gave Los Alamos the go-ahead to develop an even more powerful weapon, the hydrogen bomb.

Some leaders felt the new weapon might be necessary. As feared, the Soviet Union became aggressive after the war. Its army had remained in several Eastern European countries and forced them to appoint Communist leaders. These leaders took their orders from the Soviet government, making their nations extensions of the Soviet Union. Consequently, the countries became known as Soviet satellites. By 1947, the Soviets controlled Albania, Bulgaria, Czechoslovakia, Hungary, Romania, and Yugoslavia. The Soviets then cut off all contact between these countries and democratic nations. This imposed isolation divided Europe and was called the "Iron Curtain."

The Cold War Begins

Soviet aggression angered the United States and Great Britain. The three nations abandoned their plan of rebuilding Germany together. Instead, they divided Germany into two parts. The Soviet Union would control the eastern portion, and the United States, Great Britain, and France would monitor the western part. While the Soviets established another satellite government in East Germany, the other Allies helped West Germany build a democracy.

Now a new era of international politics began, an era that became known as the Cold War. The Cold War was not an ordinary war. There was no actual combat between troops. Instead, the Cold War was a war of public statements, propaganda, and espionage between non-Communist countries and Communist countries. The two major powers of this war were the United States and the Soviet Union. Both sides were extremely suspicious of one another, each believing that the other wanted to rule the world.

The Cold War, which almost immediately followed the development of nuclear weapons, was marked by a paranoid fear of nuclear war. By 1949, the Soviet Union had developed its own atomic bomb, and the chance of one country obliterating the other had become possible. This raised the stakes of actual warfare. A war fought with enough nuclear bombs could destroy much of the life on earth. This fear kept both nations from starting battles that might grow into a nuclear war. Yet both countries continued building bigger and better nuclear weapons as a defense against each other. The quest by both countries for a superior nuclear stockpile became known as the arms race.

The Arms Race

The arms race made it necessary to maintain various labs, factories, and testing sites around the United States. Hanford and Oak Ridge continued to produce fuel for nuclear weapons. But now, the people manning the machinery knew what their factories were making. The Atomic Energy Commission invested $100 million in Los Alamos, and the community began growing again. Laboratories were expanded and more facilities were built on neighboring mesas.

On November 1, 1952, the world's first hydrogen, or thermonuclear, bomb was tested in the Pacific Ocean. A thermonuclear bomb is made by joining several atoms of hydrogen in a process called fusion. Fusion releases energy in the form of heat, and this heat creates an explosive force. The thermonuclear bomb is thousands of times more powerful than a fission bomb. Such a bomb would cause destruction far beyond what had occurred at Hiroshima and Nagasaki. Like the first atomic bombs, the technology for making the thermonuclear bomb had been developed in Los Alamos.

While some of the Los Alamos scientists worked on improving the American nuclear arsenal, others developed peaceful ways to use atomic energy. In 1954, nuclear energy was used to power a navy submarine called the *Nautilus*. The first United States nuclear power plant opened in Pennsylvania in 1957. The nuclear age had arrived.

This new era brought with it a new way of thinking. I. I. Rabi, one of the scientists who had helped build the first atomic bomb, described how nuclear weapons affected the way people viewed their place in nature. "Up until then," he said, "humanity was, after all, a limited factor in the evolution and process of nature. The vast oceans, lakes and rivers, the atmosphere, were not very much affected by the existence of mankind."[12] The Manhattan Project had dramatically changed all that.

The United States Navy used atomic energy to power this submarine, the U.S.S. Nautilus.

Soon *radiation poisoning* and *nuclear winter* became household words. Schools all across America held "bomb drills" as often as they held fire drills. People built "fallout shelters" in their backyards or basements, places where families planned to live in the event of a nuclear war. The shelters were made with thick concrete walls and stocked with bottled water and canned food. The government required cities to designate certain buildings as public fallout shelters. They were identified with prominent black and yellow signs on the outside.

A Nuclear World

By 1964, five nations had built nuclear weapons: the United States, the Soviet Union, France, Great Britain, and China. The United Nations, an organization created in 1945 to promote peace among nations, sought to keep this number from growing. In 1968, United Nations representatives wrote an agreement called the Treaty on the Non-Proliferation of Nuclear Weapons (NPT). Any country that signed the NPT agreed not to build nuclear weapons. Countries that already had nuclear weapons agreed not to give them to countries that did not have them. The treaty went into effect in 1970. All five nuclear nations signed the treaty as well as several other countries. Today, all but four countries in the world have signed the NPT. Those that have not signed are India, Israel, Pakistan, and Cuba.

During the 1970s, more steps were taken to reduce the threat of a nuclear holocaust. The United States

Several families built these "fallout shelters" in their basements or backyards during the 1960s. The shelters were designed to protect occupants from radiation poisoning in the event of nuclear war.

and the Soviet Union, the two nuclear superpowers, signed a treaty called the Strategic Arms Limitation Talks (SALT). SALT limited the number and kinds of nuclear weapons each nation could produce. By the late 1980s, both countries agreed to begin destroying some of the nuclear bombs they already had. The resulting treaty was called the Strategic Arms Reduction Talks, or START.

In the meantime, some of the Soviet satellites overthrew their Communist governments and became democracies. In 1990, East and West Germany reunited into one democratic country, and in 1991, the huge Soviet Union itself split into independent countries. The Cold War was over.

TRINITY'S DESCENDANTS

Today there are eight nations known to have nuclear weapon capabilities. There are five declared nuclear nations: the United States, Russia (what is left of the former Soviet Union), France, Great Britain, and China. In addition, India, Israel, and Pakistan have both the technology and the materials to build nuclear bombs. But whether these or any other countries build nuclear arsenals, there are already enough weapons in the world to obliterate entire countries. There may even be enough to destroy the human race. The United States alone owns over eight thousand nuclear bombs, and Russia possesses ten thousand.[1] Furthermore, some experts say that nations that have not produced their own nuclear bombs could buy or steal them. Terrorists might be able to do the same.

Yet in spite of the world's huge nuclear arsenal, the United States continues nuclear weapons research. The Los Alamos National Laboratory currently employs more than thirty-five hundred people. Many of the lab scientists are developing ever more powerful weapons, with the help of the most sophisticated computers in the world.

But Los Alamos scientists are also researching peaceful uses of nuclear energy. Their work may someday make pollution-free energy a reality. Experts predict that, because nuclear power does not pollute the air and does not depend on fossil fuels, it may become a prime source of energy in the twenty-first century.

In fact, nuclear power plants already contribute 17 percent of the total energy used worldwide. Most of this energy is used to make electricity. The United States, Russia, Great Britain, and Japan are all major producers of nuclear energy.

The Manhattan Sites Today

Outside the laboratory that first learned how to harness this energy, eighteen thousand Los Alamos residents perform the same daily routines as other people all across America. The security fence has long been pulled down, and the dirt road from Santa Fe is now a paved highway. But those who reside on the mesa understand their town's unique place in history. To preserve their story, several of the original ranch school buildings have been made into a museum that chronicles the creation of the first atomic bomb.

The Oak Ridge, Tennessee, site is still operating, too. About five thousand people work there. Its facilities produce radioactive substances that are used in medicine, industry, and research. Nearly thirty thousand people now live in the city of Oak Ridge.

The base where Fat Man was tested was never abandoned, either. White Sands Missile Base in southern New Mexico is one of the largest missile testing sites in the world. It covers an area almost as large as Connecticut and Rhode Island combined. Patriot missiles with extremely accurate guiding devices were perfected at White Sands. These missiles were used by the United States in the Persian Gulf War of 1991.

The Bomb's Lasting Effects

The Manhattan Project lives on in other ways, too. Many Hiroshima and Nagasaki bomb survivors are still dying from illnesses brought on by radiation. One study reports that the atomic bomb survivors have suffered from an unusually high rate of certain kinds of cancer. By the end of the twentieth century, the number of post-1945 bomb-related deaths was expected to reach almost two hundred thousand.[2]

The bombs have caused death in the United States, too. Most of the factories involved in the 1940s project disposed of their radioactive waste by burying it in tanks. But many of these tanks have corroded, and radioactive material has leaked into the soil and water around them. Eventually, this radioactivity found its way into the food and drinking water of those living nearby, causing cancer and other illnesses. The area around Hanford is particularly polluted, with one expert calling it "the most contaminated soil and groundwater site in the United States."[3] This is not surprising. The Hanford reactors produced enough plutonium for twenty thousand nuclear bombs before being shut down in 1989.

Of course, during the early days of atomic research, no one was fully aware of the long-term dangers of radiation. Even if they had been, the waste may not have been disposed of properly. The need for speed far outweighed any other considerations. Today, the Department of Energy is trying to correct these past mistakes. Experts expect that it will take decades to contain the waste at one hundred thirty different sites. The process will cost billions of dollars. But someday these places may again be usable and productive environments.

Remarkably, this process began in Japan just months after the bombs were dropped. Today, Nagasaki is a thoroughly modern city with over four hundred thousand residents; Hiroshima's population has reached a million. Both cities have an abundance of skyscrapers, parks, convenience stores, and malls. Both are filled with youth and are alive with activity. Neither city looks like the wasteland of death it was in the summer of 1945.

The City of Peace

But the cities have not forgotten their past. In Hiroshima, a red granite monument stands at ground zero to commemorate those who died in the atomic attack. Hundreds of paper cranes made by Japanese schoolchildren surround the memorial site, symbolizing a long life.

The atomic bomb leveled the city of Hiroshima, but today it is a thriving urban center.

Hiroshima also remembers its tragedy in another way. The city has become an advocate for world peace. Hiroshima's mayor issues a formal protest every time any country tests a nuclear weapon. Peace education is taught in every school, and children take regular trips to the Hiroshima Peace Memorial Museum. There, they see life-sized exhibits and explicit photographs that depict the horrors of the bombings. Furthermore, each year on August 6, hundreds of Japanese gather at Hiroshima's Peace Memorial Park to remember the people who died because of the atomic bombs. The Flame of Peace burns nearby. This torch will not be put out until the world is free of nuclear weapons.

Most countries have signed the NPT. In addition, START II treaties have reduced United States and Russian nuclear weapons by two thirds. Yet the world is still a long way from being nuclear-weapon free. Experts disagree on whether this is even desirable. Many say that a properly controlled nuclear arsenal may prevent war.

Other people still believe that the atomic bomb should have never been created. They fear that scientists have opened a Pandora's Box of evil that cannot be closed. But atomic energy has brought good to the world, too. Scientists have developed ways to use nuclear technology in medicine and industry. In addition, nuclear energy provides many nations with a power source that does not consume natural resources. As Secretary of War Henry Stimson wrote in 1946,

YOU MUST ALWAYS REMEMBER THAT PEOPLE FORGET . . . THAT THE BOMBING OF PEARL HARBOR WAS DONE WHILE WE WERE AT PEACE WITH JAPAN AND TRYING OUR BEST TO NEGOTIATE A TREATY WITH THEM.

ALL YOU HAVE TO DO IS GO OUT AND STAND ON THE KEEL OF THE BATTLESHIP IN PEARL HARBOR WITH THE 3,000 YOUNGSTERS UNDERNEATH IT WHO HAD NO CHANCE WHATEVER OF SAVING THEIR LIVES. THAT IS TRUE OF TWO OR THREE OTHER BATTLESHIPS THAT WERE SUNK IN PEARL HARBOR. ALTOGETHER, THERE WERE BETWEEN 3,000 AND 6,000 YOUNGSTERS KILLED AT THAT TIME WITHOUT ANY DECLARATION OF WAR. IT WAS PLAIN MURDER.

I KNEW WHAT I WAS DOING WHEN I STOPPED THE WAR THAT WOULD HAVE KILLED A HALF MILLION YOUNGSTERS ON BOTH SIDES IF THOSE BOMBS HAD NOT BEEN DROPPED. I HAVE NO REGRETS AND, UNDER THE SAME CIRCUMSTANCES, I WOULD DO IT AGAIN. . . . [4]

Even years after the end of World War II, President Harry Truman expressed no regret over having decided to use the atomic bomb against the Japanese.

"The focus of the problem does not lie in the atom; it resides in the hearts of men."[5]

Whatever one believes about nuclear technology, one thing cannot be denied: The scientific accomplishments of the Manhattan Project were phenomenal. It took these scientists less than five years to make technological leaps that might have taken decades under different circumstances. Of course, much of their speed was motivated by the desire to rid the world of the Nazis. But their success was also due to the fact that they were all brilliant scientists. Each one was driven by the need to know more. The sheer excitement of making scientific discoveries kept many of them working even when they were tired or frustrated. Because of their efforts, humanity gained a great deal of knowledge. Indeed, unlocking the secrets of the atom was fantastic science.

★ TIMELINE ★

1938—*March*: Germany invades Austria.
November: The Nazis attack Jews in Germany and Austria, destroying their homes and businesses.

1939—*January*: Lise Meitner and Otto Frisch identify fission in uranium atoms.
August: Two scientists, Leo Szilard and Eugene Wigner, write to President Roosevelt, explaining that a powerful new weapon might be possible.
September: Germany invades Poland; Great Britain and France declare war on Germany.
October: President Roosevelt orders a committee to investigate the possibility of developing atomic weapons.

1940—*April*: Germany invades Norway and Denmark.
May: Germany invades Netherlands and Belgium.
June: German troops enter Paris.
September: Japan joins the Axis Powers.

1941—*February*: A group of scientists working at the University of California discover another element that will fission: plutonium.
December: Japan attacks the United States at Pearl Harbor, Hawaii; The United States and Great Britain declare war on Japan; Germany and Italy declare war on the United States.

1942—*June*: President Roosevelt orders the army to build an atomic bomb.
September: General Leslie Groves purchases land in Tennessee to build a factory to produce fuel for an atomic bomb.
October: Los Alamos, New Mexico, is selected as the site for the bomb-designing laboratory.
December: Enrico Fermi creates the first self-sustaining chain reaction in uranium at the laboratory in Chicago.

1943—*January*: The Los Alamos Laboratory opens; J. Robert Oppenheimer becomes its director; Groves buys a site in Hanford, Washington, for a fuel factory.

September: Italy surrenders to the Allies.

1944—*June*: The Allies invade France.

August: Paris is liberated; Groves chooses a site in southern New Mexico for the implosion test.

September: Belgium is liberated.

1945—*March*: Allied troops enter German concentration camps to find that the Nazis have been murdering millions of European Jews; United States forces liberate the Philippines and the island of Iwo Jima.

April: President Roosevelt dies, making Vice President Harry Truman the new president; Truman learns about the Manhattan Project; Hitler commits suicide.

May: Germany surrenders.

June: United States troops capture Okinawa.

July 16: The implosion bomb is successfully tested at Trinity.

July 26: The Potsdam Declaration is issued by the Allies, demanding Japan's unconditional surrender.

July 28: Japan rejects the Potsdam Declaration.

August 6: Atomic bomb is dropped on Hiroshima, Japan.

August 8: The Soviet Union declares war on Japan.

August 9: Second atomic bomb is dropped on Nagasaki, Japan.

August 14: World War II ends.

September 2: Japan surrenders formally.

1946—The Cold War begins.

1947—*January*: The Manhattan Engineering District officially ends; The Atomic Energy Commission is formed to oversee atomic energy and nuclear weapons.

1949—The Soviet Union develops its own atomic weapon, marking the beginning of the nuclear arms race.

1952—The United States successfully tests the hydrogen bomb.

1957—The first United States nuclear power plant opens in Pennsylvania.

1970—The United States and the Soviet Union agree to limit the number and kind of nuclear weapons they make; The specific agreement is worked out in negotiations called the Strategic Arms Limitation Talks.

1980 —The United States and the Soviet Union agree to
–1990 begin reducing their nuclear stockpiles, according to the Strategic Arms Reduction Talks treaty.

1991—The Cold War ends.

★ CHAPTER NOTES ★

Chapter 1. Mission: Possible

1. Rachel Fermi and Esther Samra, *Picturing the Bomb: Photographs From the Secret World of the Manhattan Project* (New York: Harry N. Abrams, Inc., 1995), p. 66.

Chapter 2. Discovery!

1. American Institute of Physics, "Public Concerns III," *A. Einstein Image and Impact*, 1996, <http://www.aip.org/history/einstein/public3.htm>, (August 11, 1999).

2. Quoted in Louis L. Snyder, ed., *Fifty Major Documents of the 20th Century* (Princeton, N.J.: D. Van Nostrand Company, Inc., 1955), pp. 74, 75, 76.

3. Emilio Segrè, *Enrico Fermi: Physicist* (Chicago: The University of Chicago Press, 1970), p. 97.

4. Rachel Fermi and Esther Samra, *Picturing the Bomb: Photographs From the Secret World of the Manhattan Project* (New York: Harry N. Abrams, Inc., 1995), p. 96.

Chapter 3. Alert!

1. Emilio Segrè, *Enrico Fermi: Physicist* (Chicago: The University of Chicago Press, 1970), p. 113.

2. Quoted in Jerome B. Agel, *Words That Make America Great* (New York: Random House, 1997), p. 510.

3. Robert Jungk, *Brighter Than a Thousand Suns* (New York: Harcourt, Brace, and Company, 1958), p. 109.

4. Ibid., p. 111.

5. Sarah R. Riedman, *Men and Women Behind the Atom* (New York: Abelard-Schuman Limited, 1958), p. 126.

6. Leslie M. Groves, *Now It Can Be Told: The Story of the Manhattan Project* (New York: Da Capo Press, Inc., 1962), p. 34.

7. Martin Gilbert, *Churchill: A Life* (New York: Henry Holt and Company, 1991), p. 656.

Chapter 4. One Theory Proven

1. Quoted in Richard Hofstadter and Beatrice K. Hofstadter, *Great Issues in American History*, Rev. ed. (New York: Vintage Books, 1982), vol. 3, pp. 401–403.

2. Dan Kurzman, *Blood and Water: Sabotaging Hitler's Bomb* (New York: Henry Holt and Company, 1997), p. 47.

3. Stephane Groueff, *Manhattan Project: The Untold Story of the Making of the Atomic Bomb* (Boston: Little, Brown and Company, 1967), p. 8.

4. Kurzman, p. 114.

5. John Purcell, *The Best-Kept Secret: The Story of the Atomic Bomb* (New York: The Vanguard Press, Inc., 1963), p. 118.

Chapter 5. X, Y, and W

1. Public Relations Office of the Los Alamos Scientific Laboratory, *Los Alamos: Beginning of an Era 1943–1945* (Los Alamos, N.M.: Los Alamos Historical Society, 1993), p. 3.

2. Ibid., p. 12.

3. Stephane Groueff, *Manhattan Project: The Untold Story of the Making of the Atomic Bomb* (Boston: Little, Brown and Company, 1967), p. 196.

4. Sarah R. Riedman, *Men and Women Behind the Atom* (New York: Abelard-Schuman Limited, 1958), pp. 124–125.

5. Lawrence Badash, *Scientists and the Development of Nuclear Weapons* (Atlantic Highlands, N.J.: Humanities Press, 1995), p. 106.

6. Public Relations Office of the Los Alamos Scientific Laboratory, p. 18.

7. Ferenc Morton Szasz, *The Day the Sun Rose Twice* (Albuquerque: University of New Mexico Press, 1984), pp. 17–18, 24.

Chapter 6. Inside an Atomic Bomb

1. John Purcell, *The Best-Kept Secret: The Story of the Atomic Bomb* (New York: The Vanguard Press, Inc., 1963), p. 130.

2. Ibid.

3. Public Relations Office of the Los Alamos Scientific Laboratory, *Los Alamos: Beginning of an Era 1943–1945* (Los Alamos, N.M.: Los Alamos Historical Society, 1993), p. 18.

4. Rachel Fermi and Esther Samra, *Picturing the Bomb: Photographs From the Secret World of the Manhattan Project* (New York: Harry N. Abrams, Inc., 1995), p. 104.

5. Rae Tyson and Paul Hoversten, "50 Years Later, A-bomb's Dust Hasn't Settled," *USA Today*, August 4, 1995, p. 6A.

6. Lansing Lamont, *Day of Trinity* (New York: Atheneum, 1965), p. 124.

Chapter 7. Final Preparations

1. Michael Amrine, *The Great Decision: The Secret History of the Atomic Bomb* (New York: G. P. Putnam's Sons, 1959), p. 61.

2. Lansing Lamont, *Day of Trinity* (New York: Atheneum, 1965), p. 98.

3. J. Samuel Walker, *Prompt and Utter Destruction: Truman and the Use of Atomic Bombs Against Japan* (Chapel Hill: The University of North Carolina Press, 1997), p. 8.

4. Ibid., p. 13.

5. Amrine, p. 73.

6. Ibid., p. 154.

7. Dennis D. Wainstock, *The Decision to Drop the Atomic Bomb* (Westport, Conn.: Praeger, 1996), p. 47.

8. Lamont, p. 164.

Chapter 8. Test Day for Fat Man

1. Lansing Lamont, *Day of Trinity* (New York: Atheneum, 1965), p. 169.

2. Ibid., p. 173.

3. Sid Moody, Associated Press, "What Was That?" *Fort Collins Coloradoan*, July 16, 1995, p. E1.

4. David Grogan, "Witness at Trinity Site," *People Weekly*, July 17, 1995, pp. 68–74.

5. Leslie M. Groves, *Now It Can Be Told: The Story of the Manhattan Project* (New York: Da Capo Press, Inc., 1962), p. 296.

6. Lamont, p. 162.

7. Grogan, pp. 68–74.

8. Thomas R. Allen and Norman Polmar, *Code-Name Downfall* (New York: Simon & Schuster, 1995), p. 261.

9. Michael Amrine, *The Great Decision: The Secret History of the Atomic Bomb* (New York: G. P. Putnam's Sons, 1959), p. 166.

10. Ferenc Morton Szasz, *The Day the Sun Rose Twice* (Albuquerque: University of New Mexico Press, 1984), p. 84.

11. Allen and Polmar, p. 261.

12. Quoted in David Colbert, ed., *Eyewitness to America: 500 Years of America in the Words of Those Who Saw It Happen* (New York: Pantheon Books, 1997), p. 433.

13. Szasz, p. 90.

14. Moody, p. E4.

15. Stephane Groueff, *Manhattan Project: The Untold Story of the Making of the Atomic Bomb* (Boston: Little, Brown and Company, 1967), p. 355.

16. Moody, p. E4.

Chapter 9. Unleashing the Ultimate Weapon

1. Dennis D. Wainstock, *The Decision to Drop the Atomic Bomb* (Westport, Conn.: Praeger, 1996), p. 61.

2. Ibid., p. 62.

3. Lawrence Badash, *Scientists and the Development of Nuclear Weapons* (Atlantic Highlands, N.J.: Humanities Press, 1995), p. 59.

4. Evan Thomas, "Why We Did It," *Newsweek*, July 24, 1995, p. 27.

5. Ferenc Morton Szasz, *The Day the Sun Rose Twice* (Albuquerque: University of New Mexico Press, 1984), p. 146.

6. Badash, p. 53.

7. "Special Report: Hiroshima: August 6, 1945," *Newsweek*, July 24, 1995, p. 21.

8. J. Samuel Walker, *Prompt and Utter Destruction: Truman and the Use of Atomic Bombs Against Japan* (Chapel Hill: The University of North Carolina Press, 1997), p. 79.

Chapter 10. The War for Peace

1. "The Nation," *Time*, August 13, 1945, p. 17.

2. Michael Amrine, *The Great Decision: The Secret History of the Atomic Bomb* (New York: G. P. Putnam's Sons, 1959), p. 210.

3. Quoted in Louis L. Snyder, ed., *Fifty Major Documents of the 20th Century* (Princeton, N.J.: D. Van Nostrand Company, Inc., 1955), pp. 119–120.

4. Dennis D. Wainstock, *The Decision to Drop the Atomic Bomb* (Westport, Conn.: Praeger, 1996), p. 119.

5. Osborn Elliot, "Eyewitness," *Newsweek*, July 24, 1995, p. 29.

6. Ibid.

7. Lawrence Badash, *Scientists and the Development of Nuclear Weapons* (Atlantic Highlands, N.J.: Humanities Press, 1995), p. 57.

8. Peggy Pond Church, *The House at Otowi Bridge: The Story of Edith Warner and Los Alamos* (Albuquerque: The University of New Mexico Press, 1960), p. 92.

9. Robert Jungk, *Brighter Than a Thousand Suns* (New York: Harcourt, Brace, and Company, 1958), pp. 221–229.

10. Nuel Pharr Davis, *Lawrence and Oppenheimer* (New York: Simon and Schuster, 1968), p. 250.

11. Brookings Institute, *Statistical Review World War II: A Summary of ASF Statistics* (U.S. Department of War, Statistics Branch, 1946).

12. Ferenc Morton Szasz, *The Day the Sun Rose Twice* (Albuquerque: University of New Mexico Press, 1984), p. 90.

Chapter 11. Trinity's Descendants

1. Brad Stone, "Nuclear Nations," *Newsweek*, July 24, 1995, p. 36.

2. Ted Gup, "Up From Ground Zero: Hiroshima," *National Geographic*, August 1995, pp. 98–99.

3. "At the Hot End of the Cold War," *American City and County*, March 1998, pp. 20–31.

4. Quoted in Andrew Carroll, ed., *Letters of a Nation* (New York: Kodansha International, 1997), p. 163.

5. Michael Blow, *The History of the Atomic Bomb* (New York: Harper and Row, 1968), p. 145.

★ FURTHER READING ★

Books

Deitch, Kenneth M., ed. *The Manhattan Project: A Secret Wartime Mission*. Lowell, Mass.: Discovery Enterprises, Ltd., 1995.

Driemen, J. E. Atomic Dawn: *A Biography of Robert Oppenheimer*. Minneapolis: Dillon Press, 1989.

Fermi, Laura. *Atoms in the Family: My Life With Enrico Fermi*. Chicago: University of Chicago Press, 1995.

Gottfried, Ted. *Enrico Fermi: Pioneer of the Atomic Age*. New York: Facts on File, 1992.

Seddon, Tom. *Atomic Bomb*. New York: Scientific American Books for Young Readers, 1995.

Sherrow, Victoria. *Hiroshima*. Parsippany, N.J.: Silver Burdett Press, 1994.

Stein, Richard C. *The Manhattan Project*. Danbury, Conn.: Children's Press, 1993.

Wainstock, Dennis D. *The Decision to Drop the Atomic Bomb*. Westport, Conn.: Praeger, 1996.

Internet Addresses

A-Bomb WWW Project. *A-Bomb WWW Museum*. 1998. <http://www.csi.ad.jp/ABOMB/> (July 13, 1999).

The Brookings Institution. "The Costs of the Manhattan Project." *The U.S. Nuclear Weapons Cost Study Project*. n.d. <http://www.brook.edu/FP/PROJECTS/NUCWCOST/MANHATTN.HTM> (July 13, 1999).

★ INDEX ★